WILL & I

WILL
&
I

A Memoir

CLAY
BYARS

FARRAR, STRAUS AND GIROUX   NEW YORK

Farrar, Straus and Giroux
18 West 18th Street, New York 10011

Library of Congress Cataloging-in-Publication Data
Names: Byars, Clay.
Title: Will & I : a memoir / Clay Byars.
Other titles: Will and I
Description: First edition. | New York : Farrar, Straus and Giroux,
   2016.
Identifiers: LCCN 2015041607 | ISBN 9780374290283 (pbk.) |
   ISBN 9780374714833 (e-book)
Subjects: LCSH: Byars, Clay. | Cerebrovascular disease—
   Patients—United States—Biography | Cerebrovascular
   disease—Patients—Rehabilitation. | Traffic accident
   victims—Biography. | Twins.
Classification: LCC RC388.5 .B93 2016 | DDC 616.8/10092—dc23
LC record available at http://lccn.loc.gov/2015041607

Designed by Jo Anne Metsch

Our books may be purchased in bulk for promotional, educational,
or business use. Please contact your local bookseller or the
Macmillan Corporate and Premium Sales Department at
1-800-221-7945, extension 5442, or by e-mail at
MacmillanSpecialMarkets@macmillan.com.

www.fsgbooks.com • www.fsgoriginals.com
www.twitter.com/fsgbooks • www.facebook.com/fsgbooks

1 3 5 7 9 10 8 6 4 2

TO OUR PARENTS

"Teach me . . . tell me something that will convince me. Just one word."

"One word? Okay. Ta-ra-ra-boomdeay!"

—ANTON CHEKHOV

WILL & I

1

Climbing out of my car for my third appointment, I heard a booming baritone coming from inside the house. The lesson before mine was going long. I parked in the driveway behind my teacher's truck, a red pickup with a bumper sticker that read IMAGINE BAGHDAD CHINA, as if the meaning of this were obvious. Something about the sticker, its air of competitive knowingness, had almost caused me to back out and drive away a few weeks before, after I'd pulled in for my first appointment. In fairness, part of me had probably shown up looking for a reason to leave. I'd never sung in front of people in my life, at least not since elementary school music class. I don't even sing to myself in the shower. I'm not sure why I stayed that day. Definitely not out of any great hope. Mainly it was politeness; I'd blocked out an hour of his day.

Cigarette butts, scattered on the ground below the porch, added to the bohemian feel of the house. The front steps had no railing: a challenge. But I was used to them by now. I wasn't worried about falling anymore. Still, I went slowly. I knew from experience that I needed to make sure my left toes didn't get caught under the lip of the step above as I went up. I had nothing to stabilize myself on. I angled my feet to the side, to increase their surface area.

I didn't knock—the teacher had told me not to, after the first time, when I'd interrupted a lesson. I twisted the knob and pushed the door, which more or less opened on its own. The teacher and his student were in an alcove off to the right, where he kept his piano. I turned left, into the high-ceilinged living room, where I had to sit and wait my turn.

The teacher looked like a painting I'd once seen of Bodhidharma—the man who took Buddhism from India to China—big, with a bald dome and high forehead, fringe of black hair in back, trim beard. He had an unusual name, Dewin (pronounced with the accent on the second syllable, though not everyone got it right: he told me about a man who insisted on greeting him with "How ya doin', Dew-in?"). He nodded at me and kept playing. The other student, standing across the piano from him, remained hidden, but I could hear his voice, confident and deep. And loud—the kind of voice that might break things. I don't speak Italian, but it was impossible to miss that this was a lover's song; the man was pleading with someone.

There wasn't anywhere to sit that I'd be able to get off easily when the time came. The only chair in the room that had arms (which I could push on to stand) was a thrift-store-looking yellow recliner covered with books and musical scores. There was a permanently reclined black massage chair that I didn't even consider. My only option was a low, sprung sofa. I sat on the edge, hunched forward over my feet, knowing that if I were to sit back, my knees would be over my head. I flipped through a cartoon book about suicide that had been sitting on the table in front of me.

A doctor I'd seen a few weeks before had suggested these lessons. A lucky visit, when I think back—I saw him only that once, and I hadn't even made the appointment with him, but with another doctor, who, when I did finally see her, dismissed me as a lost cause. But this other doctor, whose name I don't even remember—something ethnic, Northern accent, not from Birmingham—saw me that day and was less pessimistic. He snaked a camera through my nose and down my throat, and I sat there while he pointed at a sonogram screen on the wall, where we watched my throat muscles pulsating. He had me make vowel sounds.

"You see," he said, pointing at my larynx as I made a sustained *ooooo* sound, "there's movement on both sides." I could see what looked like two white labia in my throat, the vocal cords. They quivered vaguely.

"Your cords aren't really paralyzed," he said, "just extremely weak."

After he'd withdrawn the little lubricated tube, he asked if I had any questions.

"What can I do to make them stronger?"

"Consider singing," he said.

I laughed.

"It sounds crazy," he said, "but singing with a professional is the best way for a voice to relearn what's normally instinctive, as far as pitch and tone and articulation."

My brother-in-law, who is musical by nature, put me in touch with a man he'd sung with in college operas, who was now the choral director at a nearby high school. He also gave voice lessons out of his house.

As soon as I heard the lesson begin to wrap up, I initiated the involved process of standing, and was on my feet by the time the other student had entered the room. We politely acknowledged each other, and Dewin shifted his focus to me. "You been practicing?"

I nodded.

As I made my way over to the far side of the piano, he asked me his other customary question. Had I noticed any changes in my voice?

In fact I had, I told him. In only two lessons, I could see and feel a difference in my ability to sustain a note over a period of time (an ability Dewin had said was the only real difference between singing and speech). Granted, I hadn't seen a speech therapist in over five years. My voice had been at a frustrating plateau, and the smallest changes in it could easily become magnified. I wasn't allowing myself to get overly excited.

We had started that first lesson by Dewin simply playing the same note three times, and having me repeat the letter *K* after him: KAY-KAY-KAY. I smiled, and told him that was how my three-year-old niece, my brother's daughter, pronounced my name. Like her, I struggled with the *kl* sound at the start, tending to smear the letters together (one of the reasons people had a hard time understanding me).

As we repeated the exercise, he moved up and down the scale a half step at a time. Initially, I kept getting ahead of the rhythm—self-conscious about the slowness of my words, I had learned to overanticipate cues—but the accompaniment of a piano, and the rhythm it established, made the individual sounds more distinct. I could almost see the notes coming toward me.

"I don't know how much time you're planning on," Dewin said, "but we can straighten out a good bit of those knots in a year or two with exercises like this." Normally, I'd have heard that as excessive optimism, intended to make me feel better, something I'd become too familiar with. But I knew him a little by now, had seen his grinding work ethic. He would locate a weakness and hit it again and again. The only thing that gave me pause . . . two more years. A sentence that had become a kind of mantra to me played in my mind again: "What choice do I have?"

Dewin had deduced that part of my difficulty in speaking lay in the very efforts I was making to overcome it. That is, in attempting to maximize the volume, I had learned to "help out" the words with my body, however I could. I would unknowingly twist my jaw to the side, or hitch up my right shoulder. He explained that such straining had a reverse effect, placing a cap on the sound, and that this same instinct caused many professional singers to lose their voices prematurely. He casually mentioned a principle in physics, as if I would naturally be familiar with it: Bernoulli's principle, which involves the way speed affects pressure and vice versa. I still don't understand it well. But he said it was why you couldn't just muscle through a sound. The important things were happening in the throat, and involved tiny vibrations. He told me to practice in front of a mirror to help correct this.

We established the edges of my range and discovered it to be slightly less than one octave. "We'll work on expanding that," Dewin said. His method of teaching—saying "one more time" and then making me do five—reminded me of learning to swim, how the instructor would back up just when I reached her.

In one of the last exercises we did that day, he had me sing the word *sue* over and over, sustaining it across the duration of five descending notes. This felt to me the most like actual singing, but Dewin kept saying, "No, you're forcing it. Try it again." I didn't know what he wanted, so I tried again and got it wrong again. Then he stopped playing the piano and explained how the voice works with sound waves, and not in a vacuum. "The problem a lot of people have," he said, "is not trusting the sound enough to let the wave do the work. You definitely can hear it, too. It's like surfing."

I was there to learn to speak, but partly what was happening, of course, was that I was learning to sing. It wasn't as if singing had been something I knew how to do before the accident, and now I was experiencing it for the first time. I distinctly remember the first time I was able to sustain a note. I could feel as I came in tune with the piano, when my note and its note combined. Something else took over. It really was some kind of balancing act, or as Dewin put it, "management, not labor." The sound no longer had a ceiling.

2

I live an hour outside Birmingham, Alabama, in horse and cow country. My address is Shelby, but Shelby is mainly a historic "town" that no longer exists, plus a gas station/convenience store and post office. My house is an old barn, from the 1930s, that at some point was made habitable. It came with forty acres of land, most of it wooded, and the house sits back about a hundred yards from the road. I inherited some money in my mid-thirties, enough to buy it. The setup seemed perfect for my old, formerly stray dogs. They weren't used to confinement, and although they never wandered too far away from me, out here I didn't have to worry about them running into the road.

Driving home, I thought about calling my neighbor

Bubba, who lived across the road and generally looked out for me. I paid him for small jobs and things. I wanted to ask him to let my dogs out. But I hadn't seen him in a while, and the last time we'd talked, he'd been back working in the coal mines in Alabaster, which I didn't know he'd done before, or that such mines even existed.

There was much I didn't know about Bubba, and still don't. One day, for instance, a man came to my property to cut firewood. He'd advertised the service, and I'd called him. The wood was up on a hillside, and no sooner had he started cutting than Bubba observed him at work. Reckoning justifiably that he himself had dibs on the job (I hadn't even known he owned a chain saw), he came over and engaged the man in some kind of dialogue. I saw it all on mute through the window. There didn't appear to be any violence. When Bubba had gone, the other man, whose name was Stacey, came to the door and told me he didn't want to cause any problems, and thanks a lot but he'd be moving along. I stood and watched him walk back toward his truck. Halfway there he stopped and turned, and came striding quickly back toward me. He stopped again a few feet from my door. He looked at me intensely. "I'm not from around here," he said, "but I grew up in the country . . . Stay away from that guy."

It turned out the whole part of the county I lived in was known for its lawlessness. I learned this only after I'd moved in, and immediately realized why the land and house had been relatively cheap. The farms were isolated, on a floodplain. Cops dreaded answering calls out here.

But because of Bubba, who'd grown up in Shelby, I never had an uneasy night's sleep. Once, when I wasn't at home, the pest control man showed up. I'd known him for a while and asked him to come see about a field-mice problem. I gave him my alarm code, so he could get inside the house—I wasn't worried about his taking anything. Apparently, he forgot the code and tripped the alarm. When Bubba heard it and saw an unknown truck in my driveway, he didn't even bother to dress. In minutes he was at my door in his underwear with a loaded .30-30.

I turned off the highway halfway to my house and crossed over the first set of railroad tracks. A sense of decompression came over me. I had started to live for this feeling. It was as if the concept of time had become negotiable. Sometimes I would find reasons to go into town just so I could drive back.

The dogs hadn't heard my car in the driveway. They weren't waiting for me at the door, but were back in my room in their beds. When they saw me, the foxlike one, Daisy, jumped up and started barking as if I'd purposely tricked her. The bigger one, Jay, whimpered at the excitement.

Throughout the drive home I'd been eager for my post-lesson ritual, to sit down and listen to the CD that Dewin had made of that day's work. I studied my enunciation. It was still a shock to hear my recorded voice. When I wrote or thought to myself, I heard my old voice in my head, and really I'd never talked that much anyway. I put the CD into my computer and forwarded until I found the part

I was looking for, an exercise that required me to say "Texas toast" over and over again, repeating the phrase along with a little sequence of notes. I was disappointed that my performance was weaker than I'd thought at the time. Afterward, Dewin explained, as he always did, what we were doing and its purpose. I listened to myself asking a question.

Before starting those lessons, I'd heard a recording of my new voice only once, in the years since it had changed. Through a connection with my mother, a local news station had interviewed me before a fund-raiser. That time, watching the tape, I'd concentrated less on the sounds and more on how strange I looked. This was from before I started going to the gym. I resembled an angular and unsteady hospital patient. My eyes were wide open and had an astonished look about them, and the corner of my mouth sagged. When I did focus on what I was saying on-screen, I was startled by the unfamiliar sound of gummy straining. To myself I sounded miles away and underwater.

Sometimes I have flashes of worry that I have forgotten what my old voice sounded like, the voice I was born with or first grew into. I fear that my memory of it has grown untrustworthy, that as a result it is lost. But there is a remedy, of a kind. I can call my brother, Will. We're identical twins, and Will sounds pretty much exactly like I used to. In fact, our voices were always the most identical part of us, since we usually didn't weigh the same, and we've always carried ourselves differently. In elementary school we even began to look more like older and younger brothers than twins, but people could rarely tell us apart on the phone. If you were to hear Will speak today, you would hear a crisp and effortless, somewhat hollow baritone. He sounds the same whether he's taking a business call or telling a crude joke. Someone not from the South would say he has a Southern accent, but it's not exaggerated—nothing like our mother's (we used to make her repeat words and phrases, "theya" for *there*, "sa-po-it" for *support*). His voice is sonically deep. He's a businessman, and he knows how to make it assume a tone of authority. That's how I sounded, a younger version of Will, for twenty years of my life.

Will and I went to the same college, a small school in the mid-South, in an isolated, mountainous section. A little more than a month and a half into our sophomore year, the university hosted a "Parents' Weekend." My mother decided to throw one of her "pahties." She saw it as an opportunity to invite our friends and their parents, most of whom she still hadn't met. She and my father had rented a house way back in the woods, in a kind of forest resort/ retirement community a mile or so from campus. She planned to host the get-together there. I was stuck helping her. Will had a test coming the following Monday, and he'd gone back to Birmingham to be free of distractions. I had to pick up the tent she'd ordered—though rain wasn't in the forecast—and stand at the guard gate to give directions.

The party was a fairly typical WASP collegiate party,

supposedly casual but almost formal in its progression, and boring. My older sister was there. She'd ridden up with my parents to help. But when I finally got to the party, from my duty at the gate, I didn't see her, or many of our friends. Seconds later she and two classmates came out on the deck looking sheepish and reeking of smoke. We were standing around, and someone suggested we go to a bar on campus, the only bar, to hear bluegrass.

"I have to go there anyway," said my tall, thin, dark-headed roommate, Peter. "My shift started thirty minutes ago."

"C'mon," my sister told me, "I promise I won't embarrass you."

On our way out I spotted an old friend, Amanda, who'd grown up with Will and me in Birmingham and was here in school with us now. She said that if everyone else was headed to campus, she wanted to go, too. The only question was who would drive. A boy I'd met the previous year and who lived above me in the dorm, named Drayton, from Charleston, who'd come to the party with Amanda, agreed to take us in her car. My sister left with Peter in his. My parents said they might just throw caution to the wind and join us in a while.

Autumn was in its initial swing. It was the season of brochure pictures, and the school looked exactly the way I had pictured it before I ever got there. Fat yellow and red leaves. Clear skies and chilly temperatures. For me it brought a sense of opening outward, of possibilities expanding. The others felt it as well. When Amanda began laughing for no reason, apart from excitement, no one commented.

I remember the singer on the stereo maniacally repeating the line, "Laughing, laughing, fall apart."

When we were out on the road, less than a mile from the gate, a car coming the other way veered into our lane. It was right after a bend in the road. The other driver, a girl in her twenties, had apparently been reaching down for something on the floor of the passenger side. As soon as Drayton saw her, he swerved into her lane to avoid her. At the last second she swerved back as well.

I used to try to connect the dots to see if I could pinpoint exactly where my life took what was the beginning of this detour—earlier that day, I'd felt the dreamy detachment that usually signaled I was getting sick, I shouldn't have gone to the party; or further back, I could have gone to a different college than Will (we'd talked about it and in fact never told each other where we'd applied yet wound up applying to the same school).

The impact of the cars colliding caused me to be shot forward from the middle of the backseat into the dashboard. A piece of my lower jaw broke off and became lodged down my throat. I was instantly knocked unconscious.

One of the first people to drive up on the scene was the father of a student, not someone I saw regularly, a freshman that year. The man wasn't a doctor but he'd apparently had some medical training, in the army, I think.

Amid the growing noise and chaos, he somehow realized what had happened to me and pulled out the piece that was obstructing my airway, allowing me to breathe. I used to have to try not to think about this much. The seeming randomness of it, of my having been saved, made me shudderingly uncomfortable. I'm okay with it now. But I know that if the order of cars on the highway had been slightly different that night, I would have lain there and silently suffocated.

We were on the only road that led from campus to the interstate, and cars quickly began to pile up in both directions. My parents, who'd decided to join us, got stopped by the blocked traffic. A guy I'd gone to high school with ran back to their car and told them (mistakenly) that my sister and I had been in a wreck, but that he thought we were okay. Before my mother had time to become hysterical, she and my father were out of their car and running.

My sister and Peter had saved a table and were waiting for us at the bar. It had just begun to get crowded. She barely heard the phone ringing above the noise. When the bartender yelled her name, she thought the guy was joking, and that Peter must somehow be involved. But it was the dean of students. At first, she said, she thought he was joking, too. He told her I'd been in a serious wreck and was at the hospital with our parents, waiting to be flown to the closest city. My mother got on the phone and sobbingly told her to hurry.

When my sister and Peter reached the hospital, the paramedics were wheeling me and the girl who'd been driving the other car out to the helicopter. I was still gagging and coughing up blood. In a panic, my father grabbed my mother's arm as I went by and, so he told me, shouted, "We're gonna lose him!"

Will was asleep in Birmingham at the time. He'd planned on getting up early to study. But just before midnight, he threw back the covers and jumped out of bed with a throbbing pain in his jaw. He said it felt as if he'd just been punched. He doesn't know why but he then called up my room at school. When there was no answer, he took some aspirin and tried to go back to sleep. Not long after, my father called him with the news. This will sound made up to non–identical twins, but he and I have had incidents like that throughout our lives, and other identicals we've known have corroborated the phenomenon—when his first daughter was born I felt an unexpected, biological euphoria beyond any kind of happiness, that was like waking up stoned but fully alert. When we were children and physically fighting, if someone tried to break us up, we would both turn on that person, like a symbiotic organism.

By the time he got to Chattanooga, the city I'd been flown to, they had stabilized me somewhat. I have a fuzzy image of my father standing beside me holding my arm and telling me I'd been in a car accident. I remember being scared because I knew time had passed that I couldn't account for. But that may be the result of stories I heard later. After studying me for a minute—I probably reacted somehow—Will told the rest of the family not to worry, I was going to be fine. (I don't know whether anyone believed him, but I know he didn't care.)

Amanda's femur and ankle on one side had been crushed by the station wagon's engine, which was pushed back into the car. Several of her toes were broken on the other foot. Nothing permanent. Drayton's injuries were minor.

The other driver, a local girl, died on the flight with me. I know her name but I don't want to write it, I didn't know her. She was the daughter or niece of local mechanics. I was told she wasn't wearing a shirt when the wreck occurred. That may have been what she was reaching for. She was alone in the car. She must have been changing.

Implausible as it may seem, my voice was not affected by the impact. And over the next few weeks and months, all of my injuries—broken jaw, concussion, fistula (tear) in my carotid artery, optic nerve damage—healed on their own or were healed with surgery, with the exception of an injury to my brachial plexus, the bundle of nerves inside my right shoulder. This happened when my body, en route to the dashboard, got bashed by the passenger seat. I could no longer bend my elbow. The doctors said there wasn't any way to know for sure the extent of the damage, short of going in and having a look. But they wanted to give the nerve a chance to heal on its own. Nine months, they told my parents, was the cutoff time. If it hadn't recuperated by then, they'd do surgery.

I remember very little from that first hospitalization. A dream of safari hunting in Africa. And certain images.

A male nurse, with hairy forearms, standing beside my gurney waiting for elevator doors to open. Sucking mashed green peas through a straw. But I can't place the flow of any one moment vis-à-vis the others.

The test they'd done to pinpoint the fistula involves the injection of a contrast dye, and some of it had leaked into my brain. The headaches I started having rose to the top of the list of what hurt the most. They seemed to be taking place in the core of my person. In addition to a diverse low-intensity ache, every once in a while a sharp splash of pain would hit and just linger, like a brain freeze that kept on freezing. These sensations were of a strength I'd never experienced. The only things that seemed to soothe them were morphine and sleep, and morphine required the least participation on my part. I wouldn't have guessed it could be pleasurable to feel absolutely nothing, but it was as if every feeling of pleasure and relief I'd ever experienced had been distilled to its essence, an undifferentiated spectrum, so that it seemed I'd both expanded and disappeared.

The discovery of my allergy to Demerol is probably my most vivid memory. This was nobody's fault, since I'd never taken Demerol before and there wasn't a history of reaction with anyone in the family. In fact, when my father had his first knee replacement surgery, he practically lived off it. But I knew something was wrong immediately after it was given to me. I was still in Chattanooga then. I remember my body going from feeling like every part of it was being dipped in lava to having the most extreme chills in a matter of seconds. I gritted to my mother through my wired-shut jaw that I thought I was going to explode.

When I came home from the hospital, with my arm in a sling and a patch over my eye, I walked into my old room, and the first thing I saw was a sign my high school girlfriend's little sister had made for me on her computer. "WELCOME HOME CLAY, GET WELL SOON," it read. "From Ginny" was written in small but visible letters in the corner. My mother had hung it on the wall over my bed. I saw it and broke down.

She came rushing into my room when she heard me crying. "What is it, baby? Are you okay?" I sobbed that I was. "Bill," she screamed to my father. Beee-ulll. I heard my father's foot-pounding run down the hall.

Despite the excruciating physical pain I was in, I felt like a kid on Christmas Eve. I couldn't explain it. Everything was happening so fast I hadn't even begun to reflect on what had taken place. All I knew was that I was alive. I'd never felt more alive. I'd always known that I could handle something like this—had privately thought that this set me apart—and now I was proving it. I didn't want to attach some reason to why I was still alive and ruin the play.

3

My parents eventually divulged the news they'd been dreading telling me since the wreck. They both came into my room and sat down on my bed. I was sitting at my desk overlooking the kudzu-sloped front yard. They never came into my room together, so of course I wondered what was up.

"I've got some bad news," my father said. My mother sat on my bed and stared down at the carpet.

"Oh God, what?" I said, as if watching from above.

"Well," he sighed, "there's this relatively new surgery where they take a nerve out of the back of your leg, your sural nerve, and piece it into your shoulder, into your brachial plexus." (Right after I left Chattanooga, he bought a Ciba-Geigy medical book on the nervous system, and I can still hear the precise way he pronounced *sural* and *brachial plexus*.) "And the only places that do it are in New Orleans and San Francisco. Lucky for us, the man who invented the procedure is down in New Orleans." But, he said, the doctors first wanted to give my nerve time to regenerate itself. Intensive physical therapy was how we'd avoid another surgery.

"So?" I said on the verge of tears.

"So you're not going to be going back to Sewanee this next semester."

There wasn't anywhere in Chattanooga that provided the kind of aquatic therapy I needed. I could have made the daily commute to Nashville, but it was over an hour away and, with the addition of classes, wasn't very practical. Besides, Riverside rehab in Birmingham was one of the few other places in the Southeast that had what I needed.

In the back of my mind I'd already assumed that something like this would happen, that something else would go wrong, but hearing it in this well-prepared manner was devastating. My chest rose and my stomach sank simultaneously.

"What about my classes?" I said. Sewanee didn't accept credits from a lot of places. I knew they didn't from UAB (University of Alabama at Birmingham)—they were on the quarter system.

My mother said they'd already spoken with Birmingham Southern and classes from there would transfer to Sewanee.

"I'm not going to live out there," I said.

"That's good," my father said, "because I'm not paying for you to live out there."

"It's only for one semester, baby," my mother added. "You don't want to have another surgery, especially one like this that's new and eight hours long—yeah, eight *owahs.*"

Even then I knew this was in my best interest, but it seemed like I'd just moved away from home. I'd only had one full year of independence, but what a year it was. I already felt like a grown-up. I thought I was my own unattached man who could take care of himself. Will also being at Sewanee didn't count. I hardly wanted to move back in with my parents, back to the adolescent lifestyle that I used to lead. It would bring what I considered was an old and outgrown past far too close to the present.

"What choice do I have?"

"Exactly," my father said, and sighed. Then he smiled. My mother came over and hugged me before they both walked out.

When Will eventually found out, he was giddy with anger, he was so relieved. Another surgery likely wasn't going to be needed. When he discovered that he was no longer going to have a car, he acted as if that was a given—well yeah, sure. Everything was in walking distance at Sewanee anyway, and most of our friends had cars. He didn't care at all that I wasn't going to be there with them or that I might be lonely all by myself. "Boo-hoo," he said. "Suck it up, you pussy."

————

Months passed, and the progress wasn't what we'd hoped. My right hand was fine, but from the shoulder to the wrist, the arm was just a dangling extremity. I remember the nightly lightning storms that seemed to be taking place in it when the nerves would try to connect with each other. I would take the sling off my right arm prior to driving. Because the hand was fine, I could turn the key and grip the wheel, but I couldn't steer with it, because the arm wouldn't work, so I learned to drive with my left. Only on the open highway, when there was less turning to be done, could I use the right, anchoring the wheel with it.

I'd stopped wearing my eye patch right after the New Year. My damaged optic nerve had healed enough to allow my eyeball to track back and forth. I no longer had double vision everywhere I looked.

If I dwelled on the negative aspects of my situation— living back at home, having endless amounts of time, having the threat of surgery constantly hanging over me—I'd get lonely and depressed. I tried to concentrate on other things. This proved harder than I thought. Not submerging myself at all in my new college life at Birmingham Southern, I didn't make any new friends. And I didn't have any high school friends around I went to the trouble of becoming reacquainted with. I'd signed up for only two classes because I assumed my therapy sessions would go the full two hours every time, and they didn't. I went up to Sewanee most every weekend, but I still had more time to myself than I'd ever had before.

In the middle of March, my father and I went to the

hospital downtown to have something called an EMG nerve-conduction test, meant to give us a more accurate picture of how my therapy was going. An attendant repeatedly stuck a long, acupuncture-thin needle down into my nerves, asking me to move my arm. It didn't hurt. Later, the Japanese doctor who deciphered the results presented the news to us with a big smile. The test had shown that my nerves were indeed regenerating. My father chuckled, as if to say, "See, I told you therapy would work." I was happy and relieved, too, but on some level remained skeptical. Just because my nerves had regenerated a little didn't mean they would regenerate all the way, not a small distinction when you can't move your elbow. The nine-month mark, at which we'd need to decide about whether to operate, was approaching. Nevertheless, I smiled along with them.

4

—

A girl I'd known, whom I'd met on an outdoor hiking-and-camping course after high school, came to visit a couple of weekends after that test. Her trip had been marked on my calendar for a while. It had done more than anything to keep me from getting completely depressed during the previous few months.

Eleanor was from Illinois. I hadn't seen her since Alaska, almost two years before. We kept in touch for a while afterward, then lost touch, then started communicating again after the wreck. Eleanor was two years younger, and had been the only girl in the instructorless "small group" we had broken off into for the last week of the course. It was five guys and her. We'd all become good friends by then, which is undoubtedly why the instructors put us together. You get to know someone pretty well when you spend twenty-four hours a day with them without any distractions for an entire month—things friends normally don't know, or want to know, about each other. Bathroom things. Still, her boyfriend was reluctant about her coming to visit another guy. But she didn't tell me this until after she was in Birmingham.

My first thought when I went to pick her up at the airport was how much lighter and fluffier her hair was when it was clean. Otherwise it seemed no time had passed since that summer. We hugged over my sling.

"Hi, there," she shyly said. I don't think either of us could have stopped smiling if we'd wanted.

We both agreed it had been too long.

We hugged again. Her perfume made me a little dizzy, but I didn't care. She patted my sling as we rode down the escalator to the baggage claim. "I can't believe all you've been through, Clay. I wish there was something I could have done."

Eleanor had long legs and a mixture of shyness and self-confidence you see in girls who discover only after puberty that they are attractive. She'd told us she was a tomboy when she was little, and she still had an assertive manner. The night we'd hiked out of the woods, after the course, just as I'd fallen asleep in the hayloft where we were sleeping, she had leaned over and kissed me, something no one had ever done out of the blue like that before. Her sleeping bag was next to mine, but it took a second before I realized whose hair hung in my face. I instinctively flinched and then gladly went with it.

The first night of her visit, after we'd watched a movie in the playroom and tried to call the other guys from our camping group, I told her that I was going to bed. I noticed, or thought I did anyway, that my statement had upset her. So as if I had no choice, I turned and walked over to where she was sitting on the red leather couch. I said, "Do you mind if I kiss you good night?" She smiled and said she didn't.

"What took you so long?" she said, after I sat down beside her.

I was instantly relieved but defensively replied, "I thought you had a boyfriend."

"I know." She frowned. "It's just so good to see you."

After kissing some more, I said, "I don't have a problem with it if you don't."

"Let's go upstairs," she said.

In retrospect, I get a certain pleasure from thinking that we walked hand in hand right past my parents' bedroom door, on the way up. At the time, I forgot that I had parents. My heartbeat didn't slow down until she walked out of the bathroom and into my sister's bedroom. I was already in the bed, naked and I'm sure with a hard-on. It was only when she laughed at her attempt to cover her breasts as she crossed the room that I calmed down and shifted to autopilot. Nothing felt illicit about this. And there wasn't that moment of hesitation that can come when you're initially confronted with a separate body. Because we knew each other as well as we did, my guiding principle had become forgiveness. We were in this together and whatever was okay. Her laugh echoed that. There was definitely desire—my hormones were raging—but it was secondary to a feeling of unity. I knew she felt the same way, even if she did have a boyfriend. So when I asked if she wanted to have sex and she said, "I don't know, do you?" I couldn't help but look down and laugh. We quickly went over our brief sexual pasts. Then she said, "Pull out before."

Eleanor started crying at the airport before her flight home, but it didn't make me sad. We made plans for a return visit that summer. I kept thinking, could I really be this lucky? I walked around in a daze, dividing my time between fretting over surgery and wondering about her. But as time wore on, our phone calls dwindled. She was spending more time with her boyfriend, and it was probably awkward for her to squeeze me in. And then as the surgery began to seem more and more inevitable, I became preoccupied with it, and thought about her less.

My mother was completely against the surgery from the beginning. She accepted that it was my choice but said with finality, "This thing is just too new, Clay. You have nothing to go on. I mean, who is this guy anyway?" This guy was one of the most respected surgeons in the country.

I tried to remain calm, and looked to my father for support. "Mom, he's done plenty of these operations. If it comes to that. It may not. I'm not worried at all." I was terrified.

Strangely, however, Will and I never discussed whether I should go through with the surgery. His fear for what might happen to me instinctively made him want to side with our mother, I could tell. But he knew what I had to do, what he would have been reluctant about but done himself.

This guy, Dr. Jeffrey Cohen, the neurosurgeon, was a short, later-middle-aged man with beady eyes, a bulbous nose, and prominent incisors. He had black hair with a widow's peak that he kept combed back. The edges were peppered with gray. It kind of disturbed me that he acted as if I were irrelevant as he examined me—all he wanted was my injury—but he had a crowd of interns making his rounds with him, and he immediately put me at ease by his confidence in everything he said and did.

"You see the lack of response from the biceps and deltoids, and the minimal response from the triceps and hand?" He held up my arm and had me try to move various muscles. "This is indicative of C-6 damage, and judging by the movement the patient exhibits, the damage is likely near the root."

Whenever a doctor spoke objectively about things concerning me that I knew about as sensations, but didn't have the terminology for, I felt that much more removed from my body, which was both eerie and a relief.

A young Asian woman wearing thick, oversized glasses and a lab coat looked up from the notepad she'd been writing in. "So surgery is the proper course of action here?" she said.

My pulse quickened. I glanced at my father, who looked

as anxious as I was. The interns eagerly waited Dr. Cohen's response, and to learn if they should be envious or disdainful of their peer.

He didn't answer her. He looked at his own notepad instead. "Seven o'clock Monday," he said and began walking off. My chest sank—there it was, the dreaded articulation.

"Okay," my father said, "let's do it."

As the interns began to file out into the hall behind the doctor, a shy girl in back came up to show us where I needed to go for tests and to get everything in order. One of the many forms I had to fill out asked for my consent to death being a possible outcome of the surgery. This made me pause. I knew it was just a formality, and I should have known it was coming, but seeing it in writing was a reality I wasn't prepared for.

I had another nerve-conduction test that afternoon, Friday, which turned out exactly as the doctor had said. I was then given the weekend to convince myself there was nothing to worry about. The daze I felt now lacked the airy uncertainty it had possessed before. It was more sluggish dread. I thought about death-row inmates, how their legs sometimes refuse to work at the end.

In New Orleans, where the surgery was to take place, we stayed in a family friend's condo. He was a lawyer in Birmingham, but his firm did a lot of business in New Orleans. The condo, on Conti Street, was in a relatively docile area of the French Quarter. My father made reservations for the three of us at Commander's Palace, where we sometimes used to eat after visiting friends on the Mississippi coast. I had snapper soup and oysters Bienville. Midway through the dinner, I noticed my mother staring at a man wearing ungainly shorts and a jacket, which the restaurant had apparently provided. I could tell she was worried about my surgery. Her look was not condescending, just curious. She turned to me and smiled. "Just think, you'll be all done by this time Monday. Will wants us to call him the minute it's ovah."

I knew a fraction of what Will was feeling. He was born with what we always said was a hole in his heart. The "hole" was actually a valve that hadn't properly developed. When we were in the second grade, he had to have a heart catheterization to make sure it was opening properly. Standing under the jungle gym on the elementary school playground, realizing his operation was about to start, I'd felt painfully helpless. And that was just an exploratory procedure.

After we were born, the doctors took blood out of me and gave it to him. He gave some of it back just before I left for New Orleans. I donated then as well. Having our blood on hand was purely precautionary, in case I needed it during the surgery. We each had to donate more than a pint.

I tried to sleep away the last day to speed things up. I was ready. I drifted off for about fifteen minutes once or twice but spent most of the time looking around the dimly lit room, getting mad because I couldn't fall asleep. I got up and showered at three o'clock on Monday morning.

Then I sat shivering in front of the TV, watching the last of the late show reruns followed by a local variety show. When the early morning news came on, I knew the end was near. I was delirious with fatigue by the time we arrived at the hospital.

An attendant met us at the sign-in desk and took us to a holding room where I had to strip, "even underclothes," and put on a hospital gown, and he put a bracelet on my wrist. My father asked the guy when they were going to shave my head—meant as a joke—but the guy just said he didn't think they would be shaving my head at all. As I waited for them to wheel me down to the operating room, I became a boxer about to enter the ring. I transformed into my martial, beyond-justification state of mind. I felt like beating my chest.

The last thing I remember is looking at all these aqua-green scrubs scurrying around the operating room. I knew this was serious because the doctors had on the square hats they don't wear in public. One of them leaned over me and snapped fingers. I tilted my head back to see if the IV bag had begun to drip. I closed my eyes to hurry it along. I thought about a journal entry I'd written before leaving Birmingham, meant to psych myself up for the operation, but now it seemed to dissolve into utter nonsense.

Well, my day of reckoning is here, and as many ways as I try to justify my right to life and put my next days in an optimistic perspective, the reality of physical pain and the passage of time will still be upon me. Frankly, I'm scared; actually terrified, but this fright is somewhat eased by the power of choice. It is my choice to have surgery, and whatever the outcome I have to be content and accepting. So, now faith and hope are heavy upon me; what else do I have? . . . what else does anyone have for that matter? Maybe Alaska.

5

I survived the surgery, but after my parents had given me a couple of days to wake up all the way, they let me know that Dr. Cohen had lowered my chances of total recovery to 60 percent, based on what he'd seen in my shoulder. Not wanting to alarm me, they neglected to mention that he had accidentally nicked an artery during the procedure. But he'd clamped it shut before any serious bleeding occurred. At the post-op follow-up visit, I checked out fine. I was good to go, they said. I should have been disappointed about the 60 percent prognosis, but I felt a kind of ecstasy instead. It was like when I'd gotten out of the hospital the first time, that animalistic rapture at being alive. Whether or not my arm was ever the same, I wasn't dead.

On Thursday morning I woke up at home with the sun slanting through my bedroom window in separate rays. I caught an occasional whiff of antiseptically soaked gauze mixed with the smell of my clean sheets, but if I didn't move I could almost imagine it had all been a dream. Except I didn't want it to be a dream, because then Eleanor's visit would have to be one, too. I wanted to call her right then, to wake her up. I reminded myself I was no longer racing the clock.

The phone rang, and I threw back the covers to try to answer it before my mother could, assuming it was someone calling to check on me. When I stood up, I became dizzy and spots splotched my eyes. I sat back down on the bed. I heard my mother talking and could tell by her businesslike tone that it wasn't for or about me. A moment later she appeared in my room and asked me how I felt. Fine. She told me she had to run out but would hurry back.

My unshakably bright mood persisted as I walked to get some writing paper from the den. I needed to send a lot of thank-you notes. As I searched through the drawers, a wave of intense dizziness washed over and threw me off balance. Whatever it was felt like an inhuman force, so unfamiliar it was somehow mechanical. It wasn't even within the range of anything I'd felt before. I put both hands on the desk to brace myself, but when I leaned back in the chair the dizziness left. I sat there until my heartbeat slowed somewhat. I then remembered one of the interns in New Orleans saying how important it was to eat regular meals following surgery.

I headed for the kitchen. My grandmother O'mama stood in the doorway to the garage, shaking her keys. Once inside, she immediately opened her arms. She had on a church suit, and her pocketbook dangled from her wrist.

"Our worries are finished," she announced. "You have made it."

I laughed. "I'm all here," I said.

"Yes, Clayboy," she said and petted me. "You certainly are."

O'mama was on her way to a friend's funeral but she wanted to come see me first. Her friend was living in a nursing home, where she herself wouldn't think of living, but had gone on a cruise with her daughter's family and had a stroke. "Right there on the deck of the ship," O'mama said, trying not to sound amused.

"I'll come back and sit with you when it's ovah," she said. "I mean, if that's all right."

"Well, I was going to a movie with Emily Major [Amanda's mother] this afternoon. What time will you be done?"

"Go on," she immediately said. She then reiterated, like a woman used to, and almost pleased by, having to defer her plans, "No, go on. I don't know how long the service will be, so go on and maybe I'll come back this evening. We'll have more time then anyway." She smiled wide. "Oh!" she said, and clapped her hands like a baby. "This is good. I'm so happy! Things are back to normal. I can finally get some sleep."

I was walking up the stairs to the bathroom when

another wave of dizziness hit. This episode lasted longer than the first, and left my heart racing long after it had subsided. I wasn't able to even guess at the source. I wondered if possibly Dr. Cohen had left some surgical device inside me by mistake.

As if in a fire drill, I bounded back down to the den to call my father. He wasn't in. I didn't think I had time to explain to his secretary what was happening. I didn't know what was happening. With the receiver in my hand I reached out and hung up with the other. I reluctantly dialed 911. I didn't want to invite bad news by doing so—I was still hoping the thumping in my head would turn out to be a false alarm—but as I was talking to the operator, another alien wave came, and I panicked. "I don't know what's happening," I shouted. "Please hurry!"

When this last wave had subsided and while I was waiting on another, Amanda's mother and sister drove up. Before Emily'd shut her car off, I ran through the garage and opened her door. "I'm not going to be able to go to the movie, I just called 911! I don't know what's happening to me!" I tried not to acknowledge my frantic sense of breathlessness while I was gripped in terror.

I told them about the dizzy spells as they hurried inside behind me. Amanda's mother pulled out one of the kitchen chairs for me to sit in. "Okay," she said. "Have you eaten anything today?"

"No," I cried, "and they said that was important."

"Okay," she said again. "You need to do that right away. Grace, bring me some bread!"

Amanda's sister fumbled a slice out of the package and gave it to me. I took a bite. As I chewed and was about to swallow, I felt my throat constricting. "Pttt! Pttt!"

Just then I saw the fire engine pull up, its sirens wailing to a stop. Amanda's mother was standing behind my chair, holding on to my shoulders when all of a sudden my entire body began to convulse. It was the same kind of feeling as your teeth chattering when you're cold—you know it's happening but you're helpless to stop it. Nevertheless, I stayed clenched. Then I pissed in my pants.

Now slumped in my seat, I saw the uniformed paramedics hurriedly clanking through the garage, one with what looked like a tackle box. When they laid me down on a stretcher I caught a whiff of some guy's pungent, musky cologne. It was a scent no one I knew wore. This moved everything up a notch.

My body had become useless at this point. I could feel everything but couldn't move. My heart was pounding. While one of the paramedics fumbled around with a stethoscope, another looked at him and hunched his shoulders. My eyes—they were all that I could now consciously control—glanced up and saw a woman standing in the threshold with her hands clutching the door frame. With the sunshine behind her it was hard to tell it was Mom at first. She looked down at me. "It's all right, baby. Everything's gonna be just fine." (Later she told me she had been on her way home and had followed the fire truck all the way from the station. She said her heart skipped a beat every time it took a turn toward our house. By the time it turned into our driveway, she said her heart was pounding as hard as I told her mine was.)

I slurred, "I don know wha's happenin'." My voice had begun to shut down as well.

Finally, just as suddenly as the dizziness had come on, my heart stopped pounding and what felt like a morphine-induced calmness set in. But nothing had been given to me, and I wasn't hooked up to an IV. I thought, "Okay, this is it. Hold on."

6

Although I was conscious during this ride to the hospital, it didn't seem to be as dire as I thought. The lights may have been flashing—I don't remember—but I couldn't hear any sirens. No paramedics hovered over. Only two were in the back of the ambulance with me. While one of them struggled to wrap the elastic band of an oxygen mask around my deadweight head, the other asked me which hospital I wanted to go to. There were three in relatively close proximity to the house. I couldn't answer him, though. I didn't even try to open my mouth. If you've ever been in an elevator or a staircase when the power goes off, there's a draining sound before the emergency lights come on. The sensation was something like that. My voice and body were gone—not just shut down but seemingly far away. The guy looked at his partner. They didn't know what the problem was. All they could do was keep me stabilized until we got to the closest ER. It's strange: I couldn't move my head, but I knew precisely where we were on the route when we crowned one of the hills above downtown and began the descent. I could feel Birmingham, but I couldn't feel my body. I didn't know a condition like that existed, for anyone, much less me. It was like having one dream inside another, waking from the first but being unable to move or call out and awaken altogether.

I feared I was losing life, I suppose, so I let life recede to a dreamlike distance. It was protection. It guarded me from losing sanity. I kept expecting to snap out of it at any second. I wanted to return home and come at this whole day from a different angle.

A moment came when they were lifting the gurney and taking me inside. I saw my father's face, to my right. He'd decided his job was to reassure me. He forced his mouth to smile—almost a grin, What have you done this time?—but his eyes were horrified.

A team of doctors was discussing my case above me. CT scan, MRI, blood tests. Later in my life, I would become used to people talking about me in the third person while I was present, but at that moment, the sensation still felt new, and I kept experiencing an impulse to respond after everything they said. My brain would send out the thought, but my face would not cooperate. Each time there was a feeling of failure. And impatience. Why was this still happening?

All the lifting and positioning of my body for the tests was done to a mannequin. Gradually I let go of any illusions about control. My frustration over not being able to move or communicate turned to apathy. When the doctors' voices starting turning to noise, I didn't fight it. A numbness took over. Though somehow I was still afraid.

One of the few coherent thoughts I recall having during those first hours was a memory of visiting my brother at college a week earlier. It was a just-in-case visit, before the surgery, though of course we didn't say that. We watched the movie *Glengarry Glen Ross*. I can't remember a single scene—that's how nervous I was. I wouldn't let myself break down my fear into anything specific, so a broad sense of impending doom overshadowed everything. And now the worst was coming to pass, and that's what we'd done with our last hours together, watch a horribly depressing movie that I couldn't even remember.

The MRI results came back. The mystery over what had happened had finally been solved. I'd suffered a massive brain-stem stroke. It turned out that during the New Orleans surgery seven days prior, when the vertebral artery running through my shoulder had been "nicked" and then partially closed, it had thrown off a blood clot to the base of my brain. My father, who'd reached the hospital before the ambulance, had been urging the doctors to check the vertebral artery, but they concentrated initially on my carotid as the most likely culprit—it's the artery that leads most directly to the brain, and I had, right after the wreck, undergone a risky but necessary surgery on it, to close the fistula. Their assumption wasn't unreasonable, but we ended up losing valuable time by their refusal to listen to my father.

I was lying on my gurney in a small room beside the bulky machine I'd just been lying in. The father of a girl I'd gone to high school with was there—as a doctor, not as a friend—busying himself with something I couldn't see. I heard my father walk up from behind me and put his hand on my shoulder.

"There it is," he said.

He held up an image with some dark squiggles in a glowing field. "This is your brain," he said, "and these are the blood vessels." Along one of the squiggles there was a bulge, about the size of a nickel, but an irregular shape. It looked like a snake had swallowed a cat. "And that's the clot," he said.

He squeezed my good shoulder.

"We'll get past this," he said.

Everything he said after that is fuzzy. I was too afraid to listen, or to hear. I remember thinking, "I don't have time for this right now. Eleanor is coming back in a few weeks." In hindsight, it seems like I must have been crazy, to have been capable of such a mundane thought at a moment like that, but it was another way of keeping control. A person thinking such thoughts couldn't possibly be about to enter a new, nightmarish reality, or be about to die.

Will came in. He wore a sarcastic smile not unlike my father's, trying with his face to downplay the situation. I could tell instantly that he knew more than I did about what was going on and that the prognosis was bleak. I also knew that he wanted to leave, the second he saw me. He knew that I was conscious and trapped. And unless he could somehow get me out of it, I wanted him to leave, too. He said nothing and walked out.

I can't know for sure what he felt, seeing me, but because our thoughts run in the same channels, I know better than other people might about their brothers or sisters, by asking myself what I would have felt in his shoes. It's the frustration of the helplessness that would have been unbearable. In another family, with two other people, it would have seemed strange or even cold, his reaction, the way he'd almost spun on his heels. But he'd done it to preserve his sanity. The feeling was: at least one of us can get out. What I could never explain to a non–identical twin is that we both felt it. I watched him leave without judgment.

My condition deteriorated. The area around the clot that was being deprived of oxygen was spreading. There wasn't much the doctors could do. I didn't feel any effects—I was already paralyzed. I didn't know it at the time, or couldn't have put a word to it, but I had what's called locked-in syndrome. My brain was completely alive, but my brain stem wasn't, so my body and brain had come to have nothing actively to do with each other. Only my eyes were still under my control. I tried to bug them forward, to communicate an exaggerated expression of what I was feeling—I am here—but it must just have looked strange. They gave me painkillers, even though I wasn't relaxed enough to be in much physical pain. I could still feel my

body, but I would have leapt at being in any amount of
pain, if it would have let me resume conscious control of
it. By that I could gauge the intensity of the fear. The in-
jections at least let me sleep. The dreams I had then have
stayed with me. They offered no mental release, no escape.
In them I was also trapped. In the most vivid, I was stuck
at the bottom of an abandoned well. It had no opening at
the top. The only light that came in was from a window
high up. To wake from those nightmares not into the usual
ecstasy of realizing you'd been dreaming but instead into
an entrapment every bit as real as the dream, or more
so . . . If I could have had, in those moments, a switch and
I had been able to move my hands, I would have turned
myself off.

When Will returned to the hospital the next day, my
mother and father took him off to a private room. They
told him what the doctors had told them, that I was "more
than likely" not going to survive the week. When my blood
pressure began to drop as predicted, my father went to
Elmwood Cemetery, near the old football stadium, to look
at headstones.

7

There used to be an ironworks near my house in Shelby that converted ore for the Confederacy during the Civil War, but it closed down a century ago. There's an abandoned hotel there. According to Google Maps there's a beauty salon somewhere, but I've never seen it. It's probably just a trailer. People do that a lot, put a sign in the front yard and declare their home a place of business. Pet grooming. There's a deer-processing place down the road called Swamp Nannies.

My house sits at swamp level. In the summer there are spiderwebs all through the woods, and mosquitoes and deerflies everywhere. I have to douse any exposed part of my body in bug spray before I go on walks, even the crown of my head. I go out the front door and to a trailhead on the corner of my land, just out of sight, a trail that goes about a half mile into the woods and curves around by a railroad bed. I have to be careful about tripping on the trails, because of the way one of my feet has a tendency to drag when I step. Especially on the railroad bed, the roots are raised up so that your foot can actually pass under them. I fell there once and split open my chin. I've also broken my collarbone walking those trails. Mainly, though, I fall without incident. I find a tree to pull myself up on and keep walking. One time I was back there with my dog Jay—she was eight or nine at the time—and I fell. There were no trees around. We were in a clearing. Jay stood still and let me push up on her back.

When I bought the house eight years ago, it seemed too big at first. A lot of rooms, seven or eight, depending on how you count. It felt like it ought to be a communal space, or for more than one person and two dogs, but it was all under my ownership, and so were the woods. The owners prior to the people I bought it from kept horses. There were two old wooden stables at the end of a field behind my house.

When I moved in, the son of the previous owner leased two acres at the top of the property, near my mailbox. He lived in a converted trailer there. He was extremely neat and respectful to the point where I sometimes wondered what he was hiding. If he wasn't working at his father's pawnshop he was always home. He never turned on the lights when it got dark, and there was always the blue glow of a television or computer screen in the windows. I never saw another car up there. Finally he moved on and found somewhere closer to work, as he'd been saying he wanted to do from day one.

After he moved his trailer off, the little deck he'd built around the outside remained. Bubba showed up asking about the scrap wood. That was the day we met. He wanted to build a shed for his four-wheelers, plural. I said he was more than welcome to the wood, that I would have had to pay someone to take it down otherwise. (His shed never ended up getting built.)

I like being able to do things I'm not supposed to be able to do. A neurologist I used to see—an egomaniacal Latin American who was also very hardworking and good at his job—once told me he wanted to do a demonstration for his colleagues, to show them an MRI of my brain, and then to show them me. Point being, you couldn't always trust the MRI. According to my MRI, I should have been more or less a vegetable, and I was out hiking alone in the woods, even if I did fall some. I was a poster child for what they call "brain plasticity," the phenomenal capacity of the organ (our understanding of which is still in its infancy) to evolve new pathways and strategies for communicating with the body, adapting itself around a traumatic event. Every time I did something like, for instance, spend a year perfecting a lightbulb-changing system—involving a long Appalachian-style walking stick with a wrist strap, a table, and my good arm—I felt satisfaction, because I was flouting science.

But the longer I lived with my new condition, the

sillier it seemed to spend vast amounts of time on basic tasks just to be able to say I'd done them myself. Also, I was learning to enjoy trusting people. I'd been forced to find out a curious thing about human beings, that although most of us don't like asking for help, as social animals we do like helping others. I've been burned more than once by having my trust taken advantage of, but not enough to make me quit giving it. The experience can be pleasurable for both parties. Except, of course, when the needier party becomes too demanding, or when the one doing the helping is pushy and presumptuous.

Bubba was too lazy to be pushy, which put me at ease, too. For all his shiftlessness, he was personable, he got people, he had good instincts about when I could use his help and when I could use my space. Also he needed money. He and his stepson soon began changing clocks and lightbulbs, things I couldn't reach despite any amount of time and ingenuity. He once cut down a dead tree in my yard. His wife, Penny, started clipping the bushes out front. She was a dark-haired, demure woman from New Jersey, about forty. I met her before I met Bubba. She and her son were riding four-wheelers, cutting through my property. I was out walking on the trails and ran into them, or they almost ran into me. They wore no helmets. She introduced herself in a voice as soft as Bubba's was loud.

I wake up early out here, before six o'clock. My brother and I have always been early risers. Our friends used to hate having us spend the night, because we would get up so early, and they all wanted to sleep. One family Will went on beach trips with started packing extra games for him to play before they woke up.

Because my movements since the stroke tend to be much more conscious and deliberate than they used to be, my decisions are, too, starting with which side of the bed to sleep on. Instead of always sleeping on one side or the other, or just dropping down wherever I prefer, I always sleep now on whatever side is closest to the bathroom. It's easier for me to get out of bed to my left—the muscles being stronger on the right side of my torso—but if the right side of the bed is closer to the bathroom, I'll sleep there. By now these decisions occur at such a speed as to make them appear unconscious from the outside, but they're not. I'm always making them. Actions as simple as brushing my teeth, shaving, and showering all begin with the question "How am I going to do this?" If there are options, the easiest and most efficient win out. After years of shaving with my spastic left hand, I realized time and energy would be saved if I picked up my good hand (the right, which is attached to a limp arm) with my good arm (my left, which is attached to a spastic hand) and did it that way. No one was grading me on style. The same goes for brushing my teeth: I use the left arm to get the right hand up to my face, the right hand for finer motions. I've also learned to help out by moving my head back and forth. With showering I had to be a little more creative, applying the shampoo to my head with my left hand, then picking up my right hand to lather it into my hair. Drying off and getting dressed I won't even get into.

Just the other day, when I was in Birmingham, I received an e-mail message saying the new cable box I'd ordered was to be delivered to Shelby, so I packed up and returned. When the box hadn't arrived by 1:00, I went into town for an hour. Of course the delivery guy had come and gone by the time I got back, leaving the replacement by the door. (In the past, he has set up the new box and taken the old one himself.) Knowing I shouldn't, I decided to try to change it out myself. This involves moving the armoire in which the ancient, tanklike television sits out from the wall and unplugging the old box's power cord. Initially, I was surprised at how easily I could make the at-least-thousand-pound piece of furniture slide on carpet, when I hadn't thought I could make it budge, but I quickly realized it was not only moving on its own, it was also leaning. The front right leg had broken off and the piece was being held up on only three legs, with the fourth bent at a sixty-degree angle. It could've given way at any second. Luckily, the fattest book I own, *The Anatomy of Melancholy* by Robert Burton, fit perfectly under the corner so that even if the leg was removed the piece would still be held up, secure until someone could come help me with it.

A lot of my time goes to maintaining my body. Another person might slack off for six months, gain some weight, then work out to lose it again. For me the same lapse would lead to a reduction in mobility that could be hard to recover from. Three times a week I drive ten miles to the twenty-four-hour gym in a nearby town, where I work out on the machines I can use myself. Most of the other members are retirees. It's the only gym I've ever frequented where I've seen cigarette butts in the parking lot. Every night I ride an elliptical machine at home. I eat the same protein-rich, high-fiber lunch straight from the pot it's cooked in—quinoa with black beans, a spoonful of sour cream, splash of pepper sauce. I cook eggs or pasta for dinner. Because I wake up early, I have to take a nap at some point during the day, especially now that my body doesn't operate at the level it used to.

I've discovered that my body can no longer take the copious amounts of coffee I used to think it couldn't function without. I don't know if that has to do with the stroke. Coffee does affect the central nervous system, so maybe. Tea is how I begin my days, chai, mixed with milk—my stomach tolerates it. All of this is preparation for sitting at the desk to write. Or read. But when I'm working on a story, my whole day changes, seems to acquire more purpose, and time, along with the idea of myself, blissfully dissolves.

Occasionally I miss the intimacy of a girlfriend—when I was starting to walk again after the stroke and kept falling all the time, constantly black and blue, I used to tell people I was in an abusive relationship with the ground—but I'm not usually lonely unless I'm around other people for too long. Most of the time I'm in a relationship with everything around me—with the weather, with the woods, with my dogs, with my total environment, to which I pay attention in a way that would have seemed crazy to me before the stroke—and this sustains me. But when I'm in a group of people I tend to feel isolated and damaged and like there's something else I should be doing. Partly it comes down to fear of "putting myself out there," sure. But partly it's that the only self I can put out there isn't me—is, in fact, hiding me, behind an idea that equates the body with the person.

I don't scoff at this. I fight down self-righteous feelings of martyrdom. I'm as attracted to physical beauty as anyone, and never had to put in excessive effort to at least be noticed before. But the physical is vital in part because it's one of the ways we become compelled to look deeper into one another, and when I'm around women now, I can feel them staying on the outside. My altered body and head-injury voice are just confusing to many people. Women who do take the time to engage seem to see me as a safe way to avoid loneliness. The combination of beauty, effortless confidence, and the willingness to look beyond seems to exist only in my imagination. And something else: the experience of being constantly judged by others has made me see others more incisively, or at least pay more attention to them, with the result that take-what-you-can-get-and-run dating holds no appeal for me. It's all or nothing, so essentially that means nothing. I don't make myself available, so I can't be rejected. If that means the absence of a sexual relationship, then so be it. As Frank Conroy says, "There is more than one way for the scales to fall from a man's eyes."

8

My blood pressure eventually stabilized, and I somehow managed to beat the odds. I, of course, had no idea I was supposed to have died, but all I could think about upon hearing the news was the difference it would have made had I known this. This thought scared me more than anything else. Although I hadn't known that the outlook was so grim, I knew something was up by the somber mood everyone suddenly began to display around me. Right after this change, my parents let a couple of their Catholic friends bring their priest in to see me. As soon as I saw the guy's clerical collar, I burst into tears. I knew my last rites would soon follow.

After the prediction of my death, Will and some of our Sewanee friends waited together over at Amanda's house.

They went in shifts from there to the hospital, which my parents never left. Something he just barely remembers from that time, but which was told to me by a friend who was there and thought the incident surreal, was when an older acquaintance from childhood named Kenny King stopped by. When Will and I were in junior high and high school, my mother befriended some of the more wayward kids who passed through our house. Some of them weren't friends with my sister, Will, or me—just friends of friends— and one of them even lived with us for a little while. After hearing that an ex-boyfriend of my sister's said my mother was a bitch, another one of those guys broke his nose.

Kenny was three or four years older than us, and the times I'd met him, he'd gone out of his way to be nice. He'd developed a gambling problem rather early in life. After he got out of rehab, he sold cutlery door-to-door to pay off his debt. This was still when it was "amazing" to see scissors that could cut an aluminum can in half. My mother bought four sets of the stuff. He started off commiserating with Will over me. After Will didn't respond, he began to talk about the volunteer work he'd been doing for a place called the Crisis Center, which among other things has a suicide hotline. He said that the week before, some man had killed himself while still on the phone with him. The friend who told me this said he got so worked up by his own story that he started to laugh at its reality. Then he stopped and composed himself. She said it didn't matter, though, as Will's expression never changed.

Upon reassessing, the doctors now said that I would

remain paralyzed from my eyes down. I was given a trache-otomy to make breathing easier and a feeding tube attached directly to my stomach. This was also when the months of sponge baths, having someone hold my penis for me while I urinated, and the wiping began. But I no longer cared what happened to me.

(What stands out most about this time isn't that I was unable to move or communicate, or that other people had to guess what I needed. But because I could still feel, the most confounding part was simply having an itch. I not only couldn't scratch that itch, I couldn't tell anyone where it was either. I sometimes will have an itch and not scratch it if I'm otherwise engaged, just to make sure I still can, but the difference between being able to do something and choosing not to and not being able to do it is like the dif-ference between going to a scary movie and being scared for your safety. Eventually, as soon as I would open my eyes after sleeping, I shut them again. This illusory control transformed into a kind of meditative contentment.)

After being "locked in" for what I later learned was two weeks and two days, I woke up. I was not literally asleep at the time. I had been moved out of the ICU and into a private room. It was in the afternoon, after the physical therapist who came to move my limbs around to prevent bedsores had gone. My sister was in the room, when with no warning I consciously lifted my right leg off the mat-tress. She ran to get my parents and a nurse. But then, she said, I couldn't or wouldn't do it again.

I don't remember any of this. Soon enough, though, I was moving my leg all the time. I do remember at some point being sort of pleasantly surprised at these new movements. I still couldn't speak, with or without the tracheotomy tube in my throat. Most everyone said it was a miracle, and that now it was only a matter of time before I would be normal again. I almost let myself believe them. It was Will who shocked me out of that. He came into the room at one point and watched me perform my leg trick. He feigned excitement at first, with that same determinedly happy face, then started fidgeting and checking his watch. "Good job," he said quickly, and left, the same as before.

These abrupt reactions of his probably seem strange. He could feel that I was definitely not going to wake up and be fine, and I suspect it was as unbearable as when he'd first seen me. He may also have slipped into thinking along the same lines as me, that it wasn't real. He was young. We were young, when this happened. We'd just turned twenty when I had the stroke. He didn't know what to say, and I couldn't speak. He left.

Somehow I was able to keep the fear at a distance, or far enough away to keep from losing hope. I didn't care how I'd come by my conscious movement, only that this thing, my body, was back under my control. Focusing exclusively and with an obsessiveness known only to the bedridden on my leg—and, after a period of days, my right thumb, which came under my slight control—allowed me to stay optimistic. All of my thoughts flowed toward maintaining this control. I have this now. I will not let this go. My thumb and leg became a landscape, a whole world. I let the flow of words around the edges of the room pass into my consciousness. "Only a matter of time . . . totally normal . . ."

I don't remember much from those first few weeks, but I remember an afternoon, noticing the light coming in through the window on one of the lower floors, and knowing that it wasn't morning. The memory has no particular meaning. It's one of the few clear snapshots I have from that time.

9
—

I've been driving to weekly voice lessons with Dewin for seven years now. I don't know how many lessons that is, but at least three hundred. After every one, he gives me a CD with a recording of the session. So I now have hundreds of these CDs, and each holds unique aural evidence of the damage my voice sustained in the stroke. I say "each" but some of them, about twenty, are blank, meaning that the recording device hadn't worked that day for whatever reason. Dewin is always having to buy new machines. He keeps a lookout for deals.

Listening to the CDs at home used to be disconcerting. Dewin assured me we were making progress, but often my voice would seem not to sound any different. In fact, these private listening sessions could be the most dis-

couraging moments of my week. I found myself despising
the sound of my own voice, suspecting Dewin's kindness
and optimistic tone. At times I thought (or feared) that the
whole thing was a grotesque case of wishful thinking, both
of us allowing my hopes to become inflated because it was
less depressing than having none.

At a certain point, after a couple of years of this, there
was a subtle change. I knew something was happening. I
knew not because of what I could hear in my speech but
by how others interacted with me. I wasn't asked to repeat
myself as often. One night a childhood friend invited me
to a dinner party at her house, and I was surprised to find
myself talking at moments with the whole table, having
grown accustomed to locking in with the person closest
to me, never quite sure if I was keeping them from other
conversations.

My relationship with Dewin grew easier and more
familiar. Gone were the days when in his attempts to get
me to be "emotive" he would give me supposedly angry-
sounding phrases such as "Dang it!" to sing, and I'd have
to stifle my laughter while trying to sound enraged. Now
we used expressions drawn from reality. My dog Daisy could
be infuriatingly independent-minded. As Dewin pounded
a run of notes on the piano, I would sing, "DAI-SY, GET in
the FU-cking CAR!" As we got to know each other better,
I realized that, like me, Dewin was confident being alone.
He described going on trips by himself, and to movies by
himself, not in a tone of complaint, but as good memories. I met his mother, a sweet, white-haired Southern lady

who showed up at the end of our time one afternoon, in a nurse's uniform. She was giving Dewin a ride somewhere. They embraced. He had a little dog that he'd sometimes allow to come in during our lessons, and the voice in which he addressed the dog was similar to how he talked to younger students, encouraging but disciplinary.

The session we had in the last week of September 2009 seemed at the time like another step in the slow progression, but listening back I hear that it marked a leap. A few weeks before, when we'd been chatting just prior to the lesson, Dewin had remarked that my voice was acquiring expressiveness, becoming less monotone. The lesson that day started with my holding the word *sing* over seven notes. The exercise started low and ended as high as I could go. With a remembered fluidity, I could feel my larynx "sitting down," as Dewin would say. We had to stop after every few patterns to let me clear my throat of the mucus my vocal cords were shaking off.

Dewin told me about his work in the past with a young boy who had a diagnosis of aproxia, a mental disorder that among other things creates choppy and inconsistent flow of speech. He was attempting to strengthen the boy's underdeveloped speaking skills. "I would ask for him to chop the *H* and stall the vocal cords against the contained air that the abrupt *H* creates." He said it was like a quarterback saying, "Hut!" or James Brown saying, "He'p me!" The boy's parents brought his speech therapist with them to one lesson, and afterward she told them that basically Dewin didn't know what he was talking about.

She said the way to make an *H* was to imitate fogging a mirror. Dewin was pleased when my own experience corroborated his theory. We tried Ha-Ha-Ha-Ha-Ha just by itself, without the piano. I'd never been able to voluntarily do this before. My muscles hadn't been strong enough.

A Russian woman, a massage therapist whom I'd met in passing at Dewin's, came in right after we started this exercise, and my self-consciousness kicked in. It wasn't as strong as if she'd been a stranger, but making noise in front of anyone relatively new was still embarrassing. I'd actually been studying Russian on Rosetta Stone since we'd last seen each other. I wanted to greet her in Russian the next time, as I walked out. I thought it would surprise her, and I'd come to enjoy surprising people that way. They met me and assumed I was a village idiot, basically. I liked to keep them guessing.

Dewin handed that day's CD to me, and I started for the door. The woman and I smiled at each other in acknowledgment, but just as I began to speak, Dewin said something to her. I should have just continued on my way, but then Dewin registered that I'd also been about to speak. He stopped and said, "Sorry. You were going to say something?" My face got hot. I couldn't think of anything else in the moment. I tensed up and weakly said to the woman, "Dŏ-brey dyen" (Good day).

She laughed and said, "Oh, yeah."

10

Telling the story now, it sounds overly hasty, but they moved me out of the hospital and into therapy almost as soon as I started moving my thumb. The people at the hospital said there was nothing else they could do, and the therapists would be best now at seeing how far this recovered motion could be extended, how many parts of my body could be brought back online. My father contacted the rehab clinic, the same place where I had gone as an outpatient after the wreck. This time, though, I would not be going to the main campus but to a separate facility at another hospital, and I'd be arriving on a stretcher with an oxygen tube in my throat.

The ride across downtown was my first exposure to the world outside the hospital since my stroke. I was truly outside only for the seconds it took to transfer my gurney into the ambulance, but I remember the sudden feeling of the sun on my face, and I remember the change in pressure of the summer air. It should have been an uplifting moment, but for me an uneasy hopelessness shrouded the whole event. There was a sense of something eternal about it. Something about being exposed to the enormity of the outside shocked me from the microscopic focus I'd maintained in the hospital—back in leg-and-thumb world—and into the actual situation I faced. I was fucking paralyzed. The ambulance felt like a hearse.

My therapists—as well as a woman dressed in street clothes, who I assumed was an administrator—met me in my new room when I was rolled in. They were lined up at the foot of the bed like a group of waiters about to sing "Happy Birthday." I don't remember anything about this initial meeting, except that the woman I'd assumed was an administrator turned out to be a speech pathologist. My father had contacted her after I didn't die. She wasn't one of the regular staff.

Before my new movements had kicked in, my father had already arranged for me to be equipped with a talking computer, the kind Stephen Hawking uses. It was to have an eye sensor I could communicate with. But now that I could use my right thumb, the sensor was no longer necessary. A clicker would be used instead.

The speech pathologist came back the next day with a briefcase. She held up a poster-sized piece of audibly wobbling plastic. It contained four rows of bold black letters and two rows of numbers and other symbols. She said that until my computer arrived this would have to do.

"Let's give it a try," she said, pulling up a chair to sit the chart on. "You up for it, dear?"

Since I'd only been able to answer yes and no, my mental condition remained somewhat of a mystery to everyone except me, and Will. I blinked yes over and over. Not that I know Morse code, but at the hospital they'd given me a simple system to work with: one blink yes, two blinks no.

Now I had the alphabet at my command. It had never seemed so ancient and sacred. I actually felt grateful toward it, as a system, for allowing me to get thoughts out of my head. At last I could demonstrate my mental alertness.

The speech pathologist held up a pointer to the poster, and explained that I could guide the tip of it around with my blinks. She would watch me. As long as I didn't blink, she would drag the pointer down and across the letters. When I blinked, she'd stop.

"Spell out anything you want," she said. "This is to let your mom and dad see how this works."

I paused. It was strange to think about what my first word would be. Babies don't get to do it, don't have to do it. For some reason, I thought of an experience I'd had when I was eighteen, on the camping-and-hiking trip where I'd first met Eleanor. We were about to climb six thousand feet over a distance of ten miles. None of us had yet become used to the sixty-plus-pound packs we were carrying. Dread and skepticism showed on everyone's face. Right before we set out, a girl from Connecticut had said, "You know what Nietzsche said, 'That which does not kill me makes me stronger.'" I'd heard the saying before without knowing where it came from.

The woman scanned down the lines with her finger until I blinked, then she moved across the line until I blinked again. She would call out each letter to confirm it.

"N?" Blink.

"I?" Blink.

"E?" Blink.

"T?" Blink.

"Z??" Blink.

"S???" Blink.

She stopped and looked up at my parents. "Very good," she said with patently false enthusiasm. "So you all see how this is supposed to work?" I don't know what she really thought. That I was just randomly selecting letters?

My mother jumped in. "Nee-chee?"

I blinked, as proud of her as I knew she was of herself.

As I spelled out the quote, which began to seem longer than I'd remembered at about the fourth word, they started guessing each word before I finished, which sped things up, but also diminished the effect somewhat. After I finished, everyone just stood there. I realized I hadn't thought it through. I burst into tears, not so much because I was sad but because it would put a stop to the awkward silence I'd created. But I could see on people's faces that the quote had impacted them, and I knew they'd be tell-

ing others what I'd said. For some reason this made me
cry even harder.

When things began to settle down, the pathologist spoke
up. "The computer works this same way, except indepen-
dently. There's a cursor that moves down the lines, then
across the letters. There's also a feature that lets you enter
up to ten different phrases it will repeat by a single click.
So be thinking of things you'll be repeating. We can load
them on when the computer gets here."

Still smiling, she looked at her watch. Then she walked
over and picked up her briefcase from the windowsill.
"I'm supposed to be at Health South in five minutes," she
said to my parents. "I'll come back in five to seven days
when the computer comes in. Until then, you have my
number if you need me."

She tapped my foot on the way out. "Remember this,"
she said quietly.

11

―

Candy was a tall dark-brown woman who'd worked for one of my previous doctor's patients. The doctor gave my parents her name. She appeared on the scene sometime in those first weeks at rehab. I don't remember much about her first day, except that when she approached the bed and looked down at me, she asked, "What's going on?" as if I could answer. I figured she was another in a line of temporary sitters I'd watched pass, and that may have been the case had I not told my parents I didn't dislike her.

Candy wasn't a licensed nurse, but she knew more than a lot of the RNs I've dealt with. You could tell she'd been at it for a while. She was a generation older than me and had been a sitter since before she was eighteen. She was open to trying new things and new ways of doing things, but she also treated everything and everyone with familiarity, as if nothing was that new or that big a deal. Her face was always poised for laughter, with a kind of expectant grin, as if she were waiting for a punch line. On her second day she came in to music playing. I'd been given the first Jerry Garcia and David Grisman CD for my birthday a few months before, and had spelled out for my mother my desire to listen to it. "The Thrill Is Gone" echoed down the hall. Candy came in and said, "Hey, man, did you know that's a B. B. King song?"

I blinked twice.

"When I used to stay up in Alaska, we listened to that stuff all night sometimes."

Just hearing *Alaska*—where I'd met Eleanor—made images of her and my time there flood into my head, of hiking over fields of boulders that looked like they'd been arranged by giants, and having to call out "Hey, bear!" as we rounded bends on the caribou trails, of walking out into bright sunlight at midnight and inhaling crisp air. The whole memory seemed the perfect opposite of my circumstances.

Candy nodded, as if she could tell that her mentioning of the place had affected me. "Yeah, Anchorage," she said. "Your mom showed me your pictures."

She was quiet. The music played.

"Your boys there ain't bad," she said. "Not like B.B., though."

"I'm free, baby," she sang, "free from your spell." I rolled my eyes in amusement.

"I'm sure I've got that record somewhere at home if you want me to bring it next time I come."

Two days later she was back again.

"Hey, man, I finally found it in my attic," Candy said, strolling into my hospital room—as if nothing else had occupied her thoughts while she'd been away—holding up the record. She set her purse down and came over to my bed to show me. The weathered sleeve had a royal blue background with a picture of B. B. King in a white suit. He was sitting on a wooden stool and laughing, guitar in his lap. Candy turned the record over to let me see the song titles. She mumbled the words as she read along.

"There we go," she said. She pointed to "The Thrill Is Gone," like she'd been briefly worried that she might have been mistaken. "And that first song, 'Caldonia,' is where my car's name comes from . . . That's what we call her."

She was smiling. There wasn't really anything we could do with the record—she knew my portable stereo didn't have a turntable to play it on. But that passing moment, of connecting the two versions of the song, had given us both pleasure. In that moment we became more than an invalid and his paid keeper. There was something refreshing—I'm almost tempted to say unique—about Candy's attitude. She embraced what I was going through in the spirit of a game, one she had a stake in. There wasn't any pressure over whether I would improve, because not to do so was out of the question. She was patient but insistent. If she'd seen me do an exercise once, she never let me fail to do it the next time.

My therapy then consisted of trying to lift my leg off the mattress, stick my tongue out to my teeth, wiggle my toes, and so on. Candy watched what the therapists did, then she and I would continue the exercises after they'd left. Like her, I didn't think about what I was doing in terms of possibility or impossibility, just as a stepping stone. My greatest motivator was the fear of staying the way I was. That was not going to happen. As before, in the previous hospital, my attention would become fixated on tracking the most infinitesimal differences in my range of motion. I was aware of the slightest angle change. Weeks went by in the tunnel of these micromovements.

Usually, when we weren't doing the exercises, I could keep my spirits up, or at least level, in part because I was developing an ability to slip outside myself. Something had changed, right after the stroke. My brain had done what they say brains do: it had evolved.

Still, I would also burst into tears for no apparent reason. Whenever this happened while I was in therapy with another patient, one of the therapists would quickly wheel me off to be by myself until I was done. I didn't know why I was crying. It was like an ungrounded storm passing over.

I would also erupt into strange-sounding laughter at anything, regardless of consequences—assorted memories, easily flustered therapists, the dumpy white nurse who Candy said wanted to be from the hood, calling her "girlfriend" and snapping as she spoke ghetto slang. I would laugh at things that weren't even funny. The therapists would reprimand me like I was a little kid, shaking a finger in my face while telling me, "You just don't do that." But I did. I couldn't help it. I still have a hard time telling a story I think is the least bit funny without cracking up.

And humor has always been the means by which Will and I communicate, otherwise our closeness would be too intense to allow expression. I think lots of identical twins feel that. Some achieve the same ends by becoming silent, which Will did whenever I wanted him to talk about what was going on.

Still, he rarely lets an opportunity to fuck with me pass. After I'd been in the facility a week or so, my computer had arrived, and Candy entered the presets into it, phrases I was using over and over and didn't want to have to spell out every time, things like "I'm thirsty." Because my tracheotomy tube repeatedly got clogged with mucus, making it hard to get the little air I received, one of the automatic phrases she'd entered was "My tube needs cleaning." One morning I was trying to tell this to the doctor making his rounds, when my computer in a robotic voice announced instead, "What are you looking at, dickhead?" My face got hot, but the doctor started laughing even before Candy did.

12

My mother walked into my room one early morning holding a cup of coffee with lipstick smudges around the rim and a croissant wrapped in parchment paper, as if this were merely another day to be gotten through. Something about her determined obliviousness instantly put me on guard. The night sitter was leaning back in the recliner my father had bought for Candy. She sat up and started putting away her knitting. My mother stopped at the foot of the bed and tried to contain her proud smile.

"Guess who I talked to last night?" She looked at the night sitter and winked. "She wants to come see you this Friday, too. I said I knew you couldn't wait."

My heart sank. How could she have done this?

"It's Elin-ah," she said, and looked at me with a now uncertain smile. "That's okay, isn't it?"

I didn't respond.

"I have to get the house cleaned before they get here. It's literally a pigsty right now."

I was too distraught at the time to wonder who "they" were, so I didn't spell out the question. It quickly became the only thing I could think about, however. Was it Eleanor and her boyfriend? And if so, was it the same boyfriend she'd had before, the one we'd cheated on? I assumed so. That had been only a few months ago.

When later that day I found out my intuition was right, a queasiness set in that rolled around in my gut, gathering intensity as the weekend approached. Eleanor's boyfriend had a relative that was getting married in Atlanta, and "they" had decided to come to Birmingham first. I knew she hadn't told him about us, about our having messed around. Was bringing him here some weird attempt to expunge her guilt? She'd forgotten about him then, so she would put him in my face now, and show him in the process that she and I were just friends. I was thinking all these thoughts and at the same time yearning to see her. Still, he wasn't actually going to come down to the hospital with her, was he?

When Friday arrived, I couldn't concentrate on my therapy all that morning. Since hearing about her visit, the same hopelessness that had accompanied my ambulance ride had edged all my activity. The fairly funny physical therapist who always wore a lab coat even said something after a while. He asked if I had to be somewhere else. Because, he said, he could hurry it up if I did. When I didn't squint in laughter along with him, he became serious and asked if I felt okay. I typed out the gist of the situation. "Oh, sorry," he said. "Let me see you raise your hip twenty more times and we'll call it a day."

By the time I saw Eleanor's head peek out from behind the door, I was nauseatedly numb. Will had gone to pick her up at the motel where she was staying. He waited out in the hall with Candy. Eleanor's boyfriend had stayed back.

"Hey, there," she whispered. In my head, I automatically returned the greeting. But I didn't even have the clicker yet—I was still on the letterboard—and couldn't communicate with her. I suppose I could have, if she'd offered to use the letterboard, but did I really want that? It would only make things seem that much more different than before. She eased around the door, leaving it cracked, and said softly, "It's good to see you again."

I lowered my eyes in response. The constant suck-tick of the machine pumping oxygen into my neck was the only reason she couldn't hear my heart beating.

"This isn't quite like we planned, is it?" She now spoke in her normal voice and smiled to ease the air. I tried to return the mood. I could see it dawn on her that she was going to be doing all the talking, and I could see her getting uncomfortable because of this.

"I finally heard back from UVM," she quickly said, her words almost shaking. "I got in. Yay!" She playfully pumped her fist. "And my brother got engaged. My dog

Samantha—you remember, the pug—had this growth on her neck that we thought was cancer, but it turned out to be benign. She's eventually going to have to have it drained." She had begun to walk around and inspect the equipment in the room as she was talking. All I could think about was her boyfriend at the motel waiting for her to get back.

I felt trapped like never before. I don't remember ever being as mad at my mother. The thing that made me mad was terrible. It was watching Eleanor see me like that, and seeing that I had transformed into someone on the out-side of her life. Now I would question my entire history with her. I released the emotion the only way I could: I burst into tears.

Her back was momentarily to me, and since there wasn't any accompanying sound, it was a few seconds before she noticed. To her, it must have looked as if someone had pressed a mute button. She glanced at the door. "Wait," she quickly said. "I'm sorry. Don't do that." But I couldn't quit. Then she began to cry as well.

She sat down on the side of my bed and picked up my cold, improperly circulated hand with both of her warm ones and held it in her lap. A few minutes later, we both stopped crying. When she stood up, I knew she was about to leave. I was exhausted and relieved, feeling as if I'd run a marathon in the ten minutes she'd spent in the room. She didn't say anything. She came up beside my head and kissed me on my lifeless lips and walked out.

I knew Will would be surprised at seeing her again so

soon, but that he also wouldn't say anything. I could hear her crying again as soon as she was outside the door. I tried to blink my eyes dry before anyone else could see me. Will came in and said that he would see me the next weekend. He was heading back to school. He saw my face and looked away.

13

A day came when they said it was time to remove my tracheotomy tube. This would allow me to transfer to another unit, the main campus, which was self-contained like a college campus. It was also closer to home, in both senses. I'd have a bigger room there and my own bathroom. I no longer needed a doctor's constant supervision.

I was used to them taking the tube out, to clean off the mucus. This time, though, they didn't put it back in or hook me up immediately to oxygen. They put a bandage over the hole in my throat, the stoma. They didn't even have to stitch it up. It formed a scab and closed itself. They'd been gradually weaning me off anyway, so this wasn't a shock. Breathing through your neck isn't as strange as you may think, either. A stoma is just another way to get air into your lungs.

Now that I could feasibly talk, which a stoma hooked up to an oxygen tank doesn't allow, I couldn't. I was able to let out only a monotonous, inarticulate whisper. But it wasn't a regular whisper, a familiar whisper. It was different. It was mushy, like trying to walk in deep snow. I couldn't make sounds with it like I used to, and I couldn't swallow without some food going into my lungs. I don't know if I allowed myself the fully formed thought *My voice will never sound the same again*, but I must have known it, or feared it, which was just as bad. I was devastated. Partly I was pouring other frustrations into it, but partly this—hearing those first nonwords come out—was the real reality check on the narrative of unimpeded progress we'd subscribed to since the stroke, that it would be "only a matter of time" before I'd be "completely back to normal." This wasn't normal, this sound coming out of my mouth. It wasn't coming from someone with a direct line to a normal past. I'd been telling myself it would eventually be okay, but this . . . I couldn't see around this.

I made the ambulance trip again, but in a wheelchair this time. They secured the chair in the back, with me facing out the rear window. The main campus was about five miles away from both where I'd been and my house. Candy rode with me. It was one of the few times she stayed the night as well.

That first morning, I had to go down the hall for the morning meeting and roll call. Candy would wheel me.

Some of the other patients walked, wearing robes and slip-
pers. They apparently all knew one another. The meeting
room reminded me of a waiting room at a pediatrician's
office. Assorted goofy animal pictures hung on the walls.
There were also ones that said things like, "Do not let what
you can't do interfere with what you can do."

Candy and I met the head therapist in the hallway. She
was a twentysomething athletic woman, who from a distance seemed to be involved in a routine that had existed
for years in its monotony. She seemed to be sleepwalking.
On seeing me, she brightened up. She leaned down to my
wheelchair with her hands on her knees and said in a
tough-guy sarcastic voice, "So you're the new guy." She
chuckled like this was somehow amusing and looked at
Candy. "Has anyone shown him around? This really is a
super facility." If my neck muscles had been stronger, I
would have turned around to look at Candy myself.

"It can get kinda kooky in here"—she gestured with her
thumb—"but don't you worry, we have a whole lotta fun."

The therapist got behind my wheelchair and pushed
me into the suddenly hushed room. A large circular table
and some chairs were in the middle. After I'd been wheeled
up and stopped in front of everyone else, a girl about my
age broke the silence. She wore a hockey-style helmet
with a chinstrap. She giggled and said an embarrassed-
sounding "Good morning."

The meeting began with the therapist asking us what
day of the week it was.

My initial thought was, *Ho-ly shit! I have entered the*

Twilight Zone. What day of the week was it? Obviously some-one had made a mistake. I flashed on the day before, when I'd first arrived at the hospital. For about an hour an attendant had wheeled me around the old stone build-ing, a former TB sanitarium, while they decided where to put me. I didn't fit neatly into any of the designated cate-gories. Spinal cord injuries and assorted elderly illnesses were the two most popular wings. They ended up deciding I belonged on the TBI (traumatic brain injury) ward. An accurate diagnosis, in its way. But for most of the people there, the words meant brain-damaged. My brain felt like the least damaged part of my body. It was painfully undamaged.

When Candy stopped laughing and told them they'd made a mistake, I was moved into one of the two rooms reserved for juvenile offenders who need rehab. It was a double room they'd converted into a single, meaning it had plenty of room to exercise. The kids who usually stayed in these rooms were serving relatively minor sentences. They weren't dangerous or a flight risk. I don't even know if they had to go somewhere else afterward and serve time. No armed guard monitored the door, though there was a nurses' station right across the hall. I briefly shared my bathroom with a young black guy with cornrows, who showed up with two policemen. I never found out what he was in for, neither in custody nor in the hospital. He didn't exactly look like he needed to be there. I think maybe his arm was messed up. Candy talked to him some but didn't tell me what they'd spoken about.

The physical therapy sessions were like an old-timey high school dance. Patients waited against the walls for our therapists to summon us onto the floor. Two-foot-high blue padded worktables stood around the room, and most were already in use.

The first person I saw was an obese woman gliding around with a surprising effortlessness, inspecting the other therapists. Her movements were graceful and fluid, almost as if she were ice-skating. She seemed to be in charge—the top therapist—and given that I had the most to work on of anyone there, she was mine, too.

I made her pause for a minute, before deciding what to do with me, which pleased me for some reason. She was friendly but guarded. Shy, even—I wondered if it was her weight. But once she set to work, she exuded competence. By the end of that first day, I was standing with her help.

Almost right away it had become clear that the left side of my body was the one most severely affected by the stroke. My left foot and leg and arm, the left side of my face—that whole side didn't work like it used to, or like I tried to command. The little movement I'd regained was spastic. My body seemed no longer to possess any natural tension, either. When I stood it felt as if I were wearing lead weights. I remembered what my former, normal balance felt like, but it no longer existed. I thought I'd get used to it, though. Mainly I was excited to be standing.

My visitors by then had dwindled down to a couple of regulars and the occasional friend of my parents. I preferred at least two acquaintances coming together, because although the conversations they carried on with each other over me often didn't include me, there wasn't the stress that came with the yes/no questions of a single visitor.

One day a man I vaguely recognized showed up by himself and apologized for not coming sooner. He'd just heard I was there. He was younger than my parents but older than me, so maybe he was the older son of one of their friends. When he told me his name, Russell Levenson, and said he was the assistant rector for one of the local Episcopal churches, I thought, *Here we go.* And I now knew where I recognized him from. When Will and I had played church-league basketball in junior high, he'd been the coach of the St. Luke's team.

I stayed silent. I had progressed to single-sentence utterances by then—breathing between each syllable—but I didn't let on. He acted like he was happy to do all the talking.

"We've had bad weather for so long and it's such a nice day," he said, "I thought maybe you'd want to go outside."

I looked at Candy.

"Is that all right?" he said. I'd been outside only once, a few days after arriving.

Candy helped me get dressed and into my wheelchair. As she started to put her jacket on, Russell said, "You don't have to come if you don't want to. I mean, you're welcome to, but I can push him."

Candy looked at me and reversed the process before

grabbing her purse. "Then I'm going to run downstairs for a minute. I should be back before y'all, but if not, he'll be fine until I get here."

Outside in the afternoon sun and noticeably drier air, Russell rolled me down the sidewalk around the main building to a black wrought-iron table and chairs, across from the tennis courts, and he sat in one of the chairs across from me. After a minute he said, "So, how do you like it here?"

I nodded and shrugged my shoulders at the same time.

"Yeah," he said, "I guess a hospital is a hospital as far as you're concerned. But you don't have this"—he held out his arms—"downtown."

Almost before he'd finished I pushed out some approximation of "I'm just waiting to go home." This sounded coherent enough in my head, but I knew by his split-second pause that it hadn't come out that way.

He sighed and nodded to himself. "I know, or I can imagine, but at least now you're one step closer."

He made eye contact. "How are you coping with all this? You've been dealt a pretty tough hand."

"Fine," I said.

"Really? I don't think I'd be."

"I don't like being here, but . . ." Ever since my arrival I'd had the uneasy feeling of being absent from school with a stomachache, but I wouldn't have told him that. Still, I got the impression he was genuinely concerned and not just doing his duty.

He considered me for a second, then smiled. "That's good," he said. He looked around. "What would you think about going over to the tennis courts? I saw some guys playing when I drove in."

I nodded and smiled, too, as if we'd decided something.

Thus began Russell's weekly visits, which lasted throughout all the rest of the months I spent at the facility. He didn't seem to mind the time, and I didn't dread it. I could easily imagine drinking a beer with him. When in one of his later visits he mentioned that he'd gone to Sewanee for divinity school, I didn't feel tricked, as if his visits had concealed a hidden obligation. There was nothing conspiratorial about Russell. He was confident enough in his faith—as opposed to religious belief—to be a compassionate human first. Even when he quoted scripture, in speech or in the letters we later exchanged, it wasn't threatening or oppressive. If I didn't see those verses in the same spirit he did, it was simply my loss.

When we got back to my room Candy wasn't there.

Russell said, "Do you want to sit up for a while? Or I can help you get back in your bed, if you'll tell me what to do."

"I'm fine," I said.

Ten minutes later Candy still hadn't come back, and I could see that Russell wasn't leaving until she did. I was getting impatient, even if he wasn't. I thought maybe if I got back into bed, he would feel comfortable enough to leave. He lifted me and helped me get situated without any problems. He told me I was heavier than I looked, which at first made me wonder if I was getting fat. But it turned out the lack of natural tension made picking me up like picking up a 150-pound stone. I couldn't help at all. He then went to the door and looked out. He must have seen Candy coming down the hall, because he pulled his head back inside and finally said he'd see me later.

Among my most memorable visitors of this period was the doctor who'd operated on my carotid artery fistula. The surgery had been in Atlanta. Dr. A. was in Birmingham to give a presentation at a medical conference downtown and came by to see me beforehand. He and my father had become friends the previous fall, after the wreck. They were both self-made men who had little tolerance for bullshit and backed up their words with actions. I think he liked the fact, or at least I liked it for him, that most people would never guess what he did for a living.

As soon as he entered the room, I sensed a rising anger beneath his affability. Thanks to the blood clot Dr. Cohen had caused by cutting my vertebral artery and partially clamping it, the intricate work he'd done to restore proper blood flow to my Circle of Willis (the circle of arteries that supply blood to the brain and surrounding structures), while at the same time closing up the leak in my carotid, essentially became wasted effort.

He had me show him what I could do then, which wasn't much compared with the last time he'd seen me. He put his hand under my foot and told me to push. Then to spread my fingers out as much as possible. Finally, he shined a pen light in my eyes and had me track his finger back and forth before asking some basic questions that required only a minimal response. Will and my father waited in the hall for his assessment. Will told me later that when Dr. A. had finally walked out, before saying anything else, he looked at my father and said, "That motherfucker."

14

Around that time a close childhood friend of ours, of Will's and mine, died in an accident in Sewanee, where we were all at school together. His name was Caldwell. Most of the names in this story I've changed, but for some reason I can't change his. We'd known him since preschool and had grown up playing tennis with him at the country club where our parents were members. Like us, Caldwell spent a good portion of his adolescence there. An impudent little Napoleon with rosy cheeks and thick black hair—waitresses didn't stop offering him kids' specials until he was about seventeen—we couldn't stand him initially. He wanted to fight all the time and would never stop coming at us. But he was fiercely loyal and reliable, a high school Eagle Scout. I trusted him with money and secrets. Yet he thought nothing of putting himself in danger if it happened to lie on the way to what he wanted. I'd already taken him to the hospital once, the semester before the wreck, when he'd ridden somebody else's bicycle into a stone sundial and bent the frame. I don't know what he was after that night.

One afternoon he came by the treatment center to see me. It was the third or fourth time he'd been to visit since I'd arrived. Will was there, too. The semester was about to start, they were on their way back to school. Caldwell gave me a bumper sticker that read DOGSHIT BREATH. He'd picked it up in Florida on a fishing trip. It was true: Candy brushed my teeth every day, but the nutritional supplements I was made to consume, though I couldn't taste them, gave me putrescent breath. Caldwell had commented on it during his last visit. Will put the bumper sticker on my wheelchair. Eventually, my speech therapist made me take it off. Apparently it offended some of the other patients and therapists. And probably her. She was a Christian literalist in most matters—she would copy in little Bible verses at the bottom of my speech exercises. She pointed out that I didn't own the wheelchair, which was true.

While the sticker stayed, though, I enjoyed it. I needed to set myself apart from the religiously happy, insane-asylum feel of the treatment center. However good the therapists were, and however much I needed their instruction, I didn't want to have to join their team to receive it. I didn't mind the Christian rock they occasionally pumped into the therapy rooms, why should they mind my DOGSHIT BREATH? But because I'd yet to pass my swallowing test and be cleared to eat solid food again, I didn't want to trouble the waters. So without much protest I let them peel it off. It occurs to me now how thoughtful a gift the sticker was on Caldwell's part. He'd known it would provide me with a tiny dose of amusement each time they wheeled me down the hall. Something about the spirit of his joke, too, I liked. It was a humor we shared. When you're in the hospital for a long time, you get sick of being seen as primarily an object of pity, encouragement, whatever; it's alienating. The bumper sticker, crude as it was, told me that Caldwell and I still shared the same world.

One afternoon, about a month later, after that day's last therapy session, Candy was wheeling me back to my room when I looked up and saw my mother and a few other people gathered outside my door. They were frowning, and when they saw me, they looked down. They didn't say anything as we approached. Candy remained silent, too. She pushed me past them into the room. The minute I saw Will sitting on my bed I got scared. Candy stopped my chair in front of him, then went out, shutting the door.

"You know it's not good news, don't you?" Will said.

My heart was pounding. "Where's Dad?"

"He's all right, he's in Houston. You know Phi Point?"

"Who?"

"You know the bluff, off campus?"

I nodded.

"Two nights ago, Caldwell went out there with a couple of people. It was really foggy, and you know how that path is."

Our school, which was in the mountains, had famous fog, which could roll in with an almost liquid density and turn a clear afternoon to night in seconds.

"They decided to hold hands on the way out to the rock, all three of them, in case somebody fell."

He looked at me matter-of-factly.

"Caldwell got too close to the edge." He waited. "His neck was broken when they found him."

I burst out laughing. Now I knew this wasn't real.

"Shut up!" he said. "I'm fucking serious!"

That made me laugh even louder. How could anything else possibly happen to me?

"You know, sometimes I really wonder."

I erupted again.

"You're an asshole," he said, standing up. "Bye." He left the door open as he stormed out.

I didn't go to the funeral. My therapists decided it could have a negative impact on my progress—one of them said it and the rest adopted the theme. I was named an honorary pallbearer.

On the day of the funeral Will came to visit with a group of our old friends and fraternity brothers, people who had known Caldwell. As soon as they crossed the threshold, it became an exercise in endurance. I knew they could stay for only a minute, but it felt like an eternity. No one could understand me, and I felt more removed from my former life than ever. They didn't know how far I'd come—I was now able to stand up for a full second under my own power—only how far I was from where I'd been. I wanted to say, Don't mind this temporarily spastic and drooling bag of skin. I'm still me underneath, but I didn't. I felt trapped in a costume I couldn't even tell anyone was a costume. How could these be the same people I'd known, and thought knew me, acting as if I had entered a permanent state of otherness? One girl told me my eyes were so alive.

Will was strangely silent throughout the visit. He seemed uncomfortable and anxious to go. Partly he was giving our other friends a chance to talk—not that anybody had much to say—and partly he was . . . I don't know. He didn't want to look too closely.

"We need to head on back," he said, before anyone else had suggested it. He looked at me. "You don't care, do you?"

15

Will uses primarily his left hand, by habit, but he's almost completely ambidextrous. He plays tennis left-handed, but he writes and plays Ping-Pong with his right. He can switch his dominant hand with relative ease, especially in tennis, something I was never able to do. Once, when his collarbone was broken, he beat Caldwell 6–0 while playing right-handed (and in dress shoes). For the first twenty years of our lives, that had been the only physical difference between us, apart from the hole in his heart, which no one could see. We were still the same internally in so many ways, I knew. But now we looked very different. Our twinship had been altered.

The kind of twins Will and I are—male-male monozygotic (two identical boys)—is the rarest form of twinship, statistically. There are more likely to be fraternal (or sororal) twins than identical, and there are more likely to be female identical than male identical. It's also true that male-male identicals possess the highest overall degree of DNA overlap. We are the most identical. The reasons for these differences are poorly understood even by the scientists (just as we don't understand why a certain tribe in Africa, the Yoruba, has an astronomically high twin rate—although in that case it may have something to do with a certain type of yam they eat). It's accepted as a myth in the medical community that twins run in families, although there are plenty of examples to give the myth credibility. My uncle, my father's older brother, had two sets of twins.

I wrote that ours is "the rarest form of twinship," but that should be changed to "the rarest form of relatively common twinship." There are some extreme forms. Apart from conjoined twins—identicals born with their bodies fused—there are parasitic twins, where one twin dies in the womb and its body disappears into the other (often to reappear alarmingly later in life, in X-rays). There are also chimeric twins, where one twin disappears into the other but continues to live. This condition was discovered when doctors found that a woman did not share the DNA of a child she'd given birth to. It turned out that her lost twin's womb had nurtured the baby. There exist "mirror image" twins, those who for unknown causes split apart later in the gestation process (a week after conception, say) and who, although they look alike, will possess curious asymmetric tendencies, opposite-handedness, the same birth-marks but on different sides of the body, even dramatically opposite temperaments. Finally, there are, weirdest of all, the varieties of "semi-identical" twins. These are twins who share their mother's genes while each having the genes of a different father. It happens most frequently through a process known as superfecundation—the mother releases two eggs, and both get fertilized, at different times, by different men—but there's another scenario, the weirdest of the weird, called sesquizygotism, which occurs when two sperm cells fertilize one egg, forming a curious three-part creature, a "triploid," which then splits apart.

Here's what I find interesting about monozygotism, the kind of twinship Will and I possess. Monozygote: one zygote. The zygote is what we call the cell created by the sperm and egg, when they join. So, it's postfertilization. It divides, in the case of twins, but before it divides, it exists there in the womb as an entity, the original zygote, the product of the man and woman. There was a moment before Will and I split apart that we were literally one being.

In many ways, our relationship hasn't changed since the wreck and stroke, and in some ways it has. We are no longer physically equal, but we are more open with each other than we used to be. My condition is a subject we can now joke about, to mutual amusement. Anytime there's a disagreement between us about a fine point of memory, he will say, "That must have gotten lost in the dashboard." Once a week, at least, I have dinner with him and his wife, Betsy, and their three girls.

Betsy and I used to date as well, when we were in high school. My senior year. I'm used to it now, but I'll admit, it was strange at first. Especially after they had kids, one of whom looks and acts more like me than like her father.

I remember the afternoon he chose to tell me. It was about seven years after the stroke. A lot of time has gone by since then, and even more since high school. Will and I were over at my grandmother's apartment watching television. When the show ended Will got up, stretched and yawned in an obviously voluntary way, and said he'd see me later. At the door he turned back like he'd remembered something.

"You don't care if I ask out Betsy, do you?"

Silence. Everything around me seemed to drop. I tried to smile to show I wasn't bothered. "Why?" I whispered.

He noticed the effect of his words on me. "We've just been talking recently. I wanted to ask her out if you didn't care. I won't if you don't want me to, but you know I wouldn't care if it was you."

I took a deep breath. My mind went straight to the basest places: they'd been carrying on behind my back! But what Will had said was true—he wouldn't care. That was just it. I would. I did.

Later, when I'd gotten over the shock, I had another feeling, a sense that I was losing my individuality (a strange feeling for an identical twin to get from his brother). Betsy had been one of my last links to my former life. Will and I had always shared a lot of the same friends (though not all). We'd even dated the same girl before.

But Betsy was part of the story of my life, not Will's. I couldn't understand how she could do this . . .

"Look," he said. "If you're going to get pissed off and feel betrayed, fuck it."

"No, go ahead, go ahead. Why would I care? I don't want to date her."

"You sure? You'd tell me."

I nodded.

Along with the competitiveness that had always existed between Will and me, there was selfishness, I knew, in my stunned reaction. What right did I have to wish the two of them apart, especially when I had no intentions of my own? Betsy had just come out of a long relationship with my best friend throughout childhood, and that hadn't bothered me. Why should this? And yet how could it not?

I was as surprised as anyone at how quickly I warmed to the arrangement. Betsy and Will soon became the main people I hung around with, when I hung around with people. After all, she knew me better than almost anyone did—even better than some of my other family members—better than everyone except him. I suppose a person could say, What choice did I have? But the truth is I enjoy spending time with them, with people who know me well. I spend Christmases with them, I occasionally go on vacations with them. I love their children, their three daughters. The only time I ever saw Betsy get embarrassed, when the subject of our having dated came up (she would say she didn't, but it looked that way to me), was when the girls found out and wouldn't stop teasing us about it. They thought it was hilarious, but they seemed to have forgotten about it the next time I saw them. Still, Betsy is someone else I can trust implicitly. With her degree in accounting, and with a little help from Will, she even manages my money for me.

16

After three months the doctors started letting me go home for weekend days. The first outing was still a good week away when a skeptical excitement crept into my stomach. I had progressed by then to an electric wheelchair that I could power myself, and I could stand a little more, sluggishly shuffling back and forth from the bed to the door of my room. But I still couldn't bend my right arm, and I couldn't straighten the left. There's a natural tendency in stroke patients for the damaged arm to pull in close to the body, so my left stayed a little crooked, and I would find myself becoming aware of it around other people, and self-consciously trying to straighten it. My legs remained abnormally weak. I would try to stand, and it felt like something was physically fighting me. In the chair I could get around, but I avoided using it as much as possible.

"Now, you sure you're ready for this, man?" Candy said as she maneuvered the chair up next to my bed that Sunday morning, leaning over it and moving it along with the joystick.

I looked at her like she couldn't be serious. Going home was the major motivation for me now. The idea I'd taken shelter in at first, that I would soon magically wake up and be fine, had faded by then—it was almost completely gone—but home was still home. It was comfort. That was changing, too, of course, the way it would have been for anyone my age. Home had become both a refuge and a confinement. But I also wouldn't be going home in the same shape I'd been in when I left. I could no longer do the things I'd done last time I was there, and I knew this meant countless daily reminders of how much ground I had to make up. When I was in the hospital, it was possible to feel the stroke as part of the larger surreality of some exotic experience, but against the mundane backdrop of home, reality would be starker. Still, it was better. It was an escape. Or at least it was mine.

My father came driving up right as Candy and I got outside. He stopped parallel to the sidewalk and turned off the engine. He then stepped out of the car with his wide, camera-ready smile. "Okay, boy, let's get you home."

It was the first time I'd been in a car, as opposed to an ambulance, in over five months. There was nothing to remind me of my incarceration. Simply sitting upright in a normal car seat while moving through traffic gave me an unexpected sense of freedom.

At home, while my father fumbled around getting the chair put back together, I saw that actually getting into the house was going to be a problem. The kitchen sat up about six inches higher than the garage.

"Wait a second," my father said. "Let me get that board we used for Amanda."

"No!" I said. "I don't need it."

He looked at Candy and chuckled. "Just how do you plan on getting in the house, then?"

Without answering I backed the chair up from the threshold. I motored forward again, hoping the momentum would carry me over, but I simply banged into the little step. I then turned around and backed my chair up to the step and, helping with my arms, lifted my feet out of the footrests. With my feet flat on the smooth concrete garage I tried to summon enough strength to push down and lift myself up and over. But since my chair was motorized, it was heavier than a regular wheelchair, and I couldn't make it budge. After a few more tries, I conceded that I was going to need help. Yet when my father got behind me to push, I started screaming at him. I wanted Candy to push me, or rather, I didn't want to give him and his assumptions the satisfaction.

My father shook his head and tried not to smile. "Damn," he said under his breath.

Once inside, the smell of home came over me. I felt nauseated. Howard, our bird dog, walked into the kitchen and immediately turned around upon seeing me and my chair. I doubt he knew who I was. If he did, he must have been even more confused.

My mother came in and said, "Hey, theya, baby? Your room's all made up for you."

When I tried to go through the doorway to the hall, my wheelchair didn't seem to fit. I got angry. I stopped banging into the frame after a minute. Then I burst into tears. I hadn't expected this at all. Having this place I'd known so intimately suddenly turn on me made everything I'd been through and was going through an undeniable continuation of my past. My mother started crying, too. She pleadingly looked at my father, who I could tell was about to cry, as well.

"C'mon, now," he said. "Stop that. See, it'll fit." He wheeled me through with less than a centimeter to spare on the sides.

My room was perfectly clean and cold when I drove in. The sheets and pillows were immaculate. I felt like a prospective house buyer taking a tour. I got Candy to help me out of my chair and onto the bed. I asked her to leave me alone and to take my wheelchair with her. After she'd gone, I let my body fall back on the mattress and closed my eyes. I opened them after a minute and, before I moved or made a sound, I tried to imagine I was fine.

I started going home every weekend. The staff at the treatment center encouraged it. They said it would make my transition easier. My mother and father were coached on how to adjust to living with a special-needs person. I'm not sure if they tried to relay any of this instruction to Will, but if they did, he wouldn't have listened to a word of it. There was no way he was ever going to see me that way.

Weeks later, when I got out of the hospital permanently, I refused to let my father bring a rented wheelchair home with us. I knew I could get used to doing without one. I was already accustomed to everything about home except spending the night there. Candy would still come every day, and she drove me to therapy.

Still, my mother got together with my by this point numerous doctors and therapists and planned a little "suhpraz pah-tie" for me there at the hospital. My sister, who was a paralegal at the time and lived in a starter neighborhood near my parents, also attended. There were a lot of forced smiles and pictures taken, but there were also ice cream and cake—both of which I could and did eat. One of my therapists made a picture book for me, complete with a rhyming story that charted my progress from the beginning. It was very emotional for my mother.

Afterward, back in the kitchen at our house, she set her car keys on the counter and sighed with finality. "That's that."

I asked Candy to follow me back to my room and turn on my computer for me. She did and said good night. I sat down, resting both of my hands on the keyboard. Slowly I began to type, using only the index finger of my right hand. I remember being impressed with myself, that I could do this, dragging my one hand around like a Ouija-board pointer.

I didn't think of myself as a writer yet. I'd never kept a journal, before the wreck. I'd always had a slight literary bent—a thing that set me apart from Will, that I liked English in high school—but writing came to me more than I to it, at a time when it was all but impossible for me to communicate verbally. In those moments of laborious typing, I experienced a sense of freedom that would have amazed anyone watching. I don't know what I wrote that night, but I know that it was the beginning of a new life, one in which I would no longer try to talk myself out of reality.

17

—

Shortly after I moved home, a friend from high school, a girl named Serena, asked me to escort her to a debutante ball, where she would be ceremonially "introduced" to polite society. Since I knew or was acquainted with many of the people we'd be seeing there—a lot of them had come to the hospital after I was first admitted (as had Serena)—I couldn't help feeling the night would be my debut, as well. I went to the barber beforehand and had the beard I'd been growing since the day of my stroke shaved off.

On that Friday morning my father called me back to his bedroom for a chat. "Have a seat, son," he said, as he picked a tie off the door to his closet. He was getting dressed for work. He'd had polio as a child, and it left him with a hunched body and uneven legs. He was short with long arms, such that his wingspan exceeded his height. But he was also a good athlete before he started putting on weight. Without his shirt on, the curvature of his spine was more noticeable. It made me remember sleeping with my head against his back when Will and I were little.

As I lowered myself down onto the rolling blue ottoman, the serious, painful look that preceded what my father took to be a meaningful dissertation came over his face.

"I don't know if you've thought about how it's going to be from now on," he said. "I hope so. But you do realize things are going to be different . . . There's just no way around that."

He paused and put his hand on my shoulder, but I began to smirk. I knew he'd rehearsed this. He started to smile with me, but instead he continued. "Some people are threatened by what they're not used to. They don't mean to be, they just are." He now looked like he might cry. "But you've got to realize that most people are basically good people."

"Fine," I said, "but why are you telling me this? Why now?"

He became defensive. "Well, with tonight being your first real time out, I thought I'd better warn you."

"You don't think I'm always gonna be like this, do you?"

He hesitated and lowered his eyebrows like he was confused. "Nobody knows how far you'll go," he said. "Look at how far you've come, and you weren't supposed to progress at all. It's open-ended, how much further you'll go."

"But you don't think I'll ever get back to where I was?" I said. I had the breathlessness of peeling off a scab as I said this.

"Honestly," he said, "probably not." Then he quickly added, "That doesn't mean you can't have a full life. Look at me."

Although this was to be my first time out in public for an extended period of time, it wasn't my first time out at all. Candy and I had stopped by the bank on the way to therapy one morning a few days after I moved home, and I decided to go inside with her. It took a while, or until I was no longer outside, to realize that everyone was staring at me, and what was even more disturbing was that those who weren't staring were obviously trying not to. Still, the most surreal part of it all was that no one would make eye contact with me. Of course, I had been looked at before, but this was different. I started to make a joke to Candy about hooking me up to a leash to walk around, but she was already in front of a teller doing whatever business we had come for. When I told her later about the staring, she surprised me by saying that she'd noticed it, too, but she didn't say she thought it was strange. Instead she advised me, "Tell 'em to take a damn picture, it'll last longer." I tried to discount the stares as the reactions of people who didn't know my story yet, but the experience apparently made an impact—I didn't go out in public again before I went to the barber. Nevertheless, I genuinely looked forward to being around people I was familiar with at the ball.

The Birmingham Country Club, where the ball was held, had spared no expense. The valet drivers had on tails and white gloves. As they opened the car doors, they seemed oblivious to the fact that they were playing a very small part in a much larger production. Bronze urns with gigantic rose, gardenia, and *Elaeagnus* arrangements lined the entryway next to the porte cochere where you dropped off your car. Rose petals had been scattered up and down the long oriental carpet that led to the guest book.

We were among the last to arrive, and both dining rooms were full. Serena's father appeared from somewhere to take us to our seats. The noise level was high—I knew right away I wouldn't be having many conversations. No one could hear me. I wasn't too fazed by the stares we got as we wove in between the tables to our own.

During the meal, however, I grew frazzled. Apart from being able to have only the crudest yes-or-no conversations (along with the occasional question requiring a brief response, which Serena would then have to repeat for everyone else), I found myself disturbingly outside the general discussion. A sense of frustration overtook me, then threatened to become one of hopelessness. From the moment of our arrival, the continued avoidance of eye contact had been disturbing. Even some of the people who'd come to see me in the hospital looked away when I looked at them. What was different? There I was a patient. Here I was . . . what? A victim?

As if I didn't have enough differences telling people to stay away—I'd stopped wearing my sling for this very reason—when the few people who did come up to speak reached out to shake my hand, it was either a straight-arm handshake or I had to pick up my right hand with my left so my elbow would bend. Either way, that usually ended the meeting right then. That was also the first time that someone shook my fingertips.

After dinner, I saw one of my father's friends, a man I'd known my whole life and who had visited me at the rehab facility downtown. I felt at first a sense of relief as he made his way over to me, but before I could say anything, he introduced himself. I started to smile before I realized he wasn't kidding. When I asked if he was serious, he appeared not to understand and told me to keep up the good work. (Repeated introductions no longer make me think twice. I learned to expect them. This was in part a bad thing, because as a result, I came to depend on them. Now that I'm improved and no longer read as brain-damaged, people don't do it as often as they used to, but I have lost the habit of remembering names, certain that if whoever and I meet again, they will reintroduce themselves. I remember almost everything else about conversations, but not names.)

The debutantes and their dates lined up on opposite wings of a makeshift runway for the presentation. The announcer called out each girl's name, followed by that of her escort. The pair then joined in the center, turned, and walked toward the chairs that had been set up for club members and their wives. At the end of the runway they met the club president and his wife. After the girl curtsied to the couple, the president's wife would tie an amethyst bracelet around her wrist.

Upon our announcement, the crowd, including the other debutantes and their dates, burst into applause. I hurried to meet up with Serena. I wasn't thinking about my walking at all, just getting there. Athletic, lanky Serena was beautiful in a white dress. We'd been on the same soccer team in the second grade. When we joined, the applause became more forceful. Some of the people stood and continued their ovation. This quickly became contagious and included everyone. As I hurriedly hobbled down the runway, dragging my left leg like it was dead weight and holding tight to Serena for balance, I looked out and spotted my mother and father. They were beaming with proud smiles and watering eyes.

I felt hollow.

18

My therapy quit showing immediate results the way it had done up to then. Since coming home I'd shown hardly any improvement. The thought of stagnating terrified me. I'd start to get scared and anxious, wanting to grab on to something, to keep my progress from receding, but nothing was there.

The smothering began almost immediately as well. My mother would have breathed for me, if she could. Both she and my father were skittish around me, not trusting me to do even the smallest things for myself. Not just them—everybody was like that. It was as if overnight I'd become a not-exactly-human reminder of others' mortality. But I couldn't take out my anger on everyone, so I took it out on my parents. At one point, in a fit of frustration, I told my mother, "Thanks for life and money." She started crying. But Candy, whenever I flew into a rage, would just smile and make me repeat myself as I grew more and more furious.

When I'd been home for about a month, I received a letter from Eleanor. I still hadn't totally recovered from the trauma of her visit to my hospital room, but she had called me a few times at the treatment center, and that had gone a little better. All I could say intelligibly on the phone was yes and no, but hearing her voice had been a shot of adrenaline. She'd talked mostly to Candy, to find out how I was doing, though one time she had asked for me. Whatever else she'd said then, she mentioned that she and her most recent boyfriend had broken up, which blotted out the rest.

Her letter was in reply to one I'd written her. She began by saying that it had been a very long, very strange time. There was so much she wanted to ask me. What did I think about another visit? She had her spring break coming up in April, maybe she could come over my birthday. Then she wrote about UVM. She didn't like Vermont—she thought it was too claustrophobic—and her parents were getting a divorce. She wanted to be closer to home, so she was going to transfer after that semester. In addition to the letter, she sent along a copy of a book she had recently read.

I set the letter down. I was filled with lighthearted ecstasy and reality-crushing dread at the same time. Eleanor had made herself vulnerable to me once. It felt like maybe she was doing that again. Another person's trust—as opposed to just concern and pity—felt within my reach.

And the dread? I was scared of how she would react to me, that she might expect to find me more or less as I'd been before, which is not what I was. Also I was scared of having more of my memories destroyed. What would we do? Where would we go? Maybe she could be my keeper for a few days.

I wrote back telling her of my apprehension. I needed to be stronger before I could see her again. She responded immediately. She said she understood if I didn't want to see her, she just wanted to see me. She didn't want me to feel pressured. She didn't want to lose touch again, though, and she thought that might be happening. But she agreed—letters could work.

Around the same time, I got a letter from Will, who'd gone to Spain on a study-abroad program—which I found out later was our parents' idea. He and a friend from Sewanee were living in San Sebastian with a guy from Boston and a Swedish girl. His Spanish wasn't that great, but his new roommates were fluent, so he was able to draft. It was a miracle that he'd been allowed to go at all. Months earlier, he'd been busted while driving some people home after a concert in Athens, Georgia. He passed a Wendy's on the way to the apartment where he was staying, and screeched into the exit side of the drive-through. A cop on patrol nearby witnessed this and pulled him over once he got back in traffic. He gave Will a DUI test, which Will passed, but then he found half an ounce of weed one of

the guys tried to hide in the back of the car. He arrested
Will after no one claimed it. In a fit of frustration, when
Will refused to divulge where the marijuana had come
from, my father punched him, and later scared the shit out
of him by convincing him he'd been given six months in
jail. But in the end, Will's lawyer was good enough to keep
the judge from making an example of him, and my mother
resumed referring to him as "my little jailbird." His letter
made me laugh and filled me with envy. He was having
adventures. He'd been thrown off a train one night somewhere in rural France—Dax, he thinks—because they
didn't have the right tickets, then almost got arrested by
the border guards at the desolate station for having im-
proper documentation. He sounded happy. But all I could
think about was how permanently far away all of it seemed.

My twenty-first birthday arrived. I was in my bathroom
trying to shave with my spastic left arm when I heard
Candy calling my name from down the hall. She knew from
experience not to surprise me and my jumpy reflexes.
There were usually ten or fifteen minutes between my parents' leaving for work and Candy's pulling up. I suspected
they sat in their car at the bottom of the driveway until she
got there, but I couldn't bring myself to check. It was the
only time I had completely to myself. In that quarter hour
or less I found a stillness that wasn't possible otherwise,
and somehow felt less alone.

"The big two-one," Candy said, and collapsed back

into the leather chair in my room. "You already had a beer this morning?"

"Right."

"C'mon," she said, "now you're legal. How's it feel?"

I didn't even have to think about it. "Sometimes like I'm the oldest person alive, and sometimes like I'm three."

She smiled. "Aw, man, it's not that bad." But then she nodded.

I went and put on my bathing suit. She and I had discussed that today would be my first time back in the pool. I'd been looking forward to it. The therapy exercises I could do in the water were limitless. I knew the water would still be cold—it was only April—but the occasion was momentous. I would be able to look back and see my twenty-first birthday as the day I began my real recovery.

We walked out back and down the steps to the pool. My weak toes made it harder to walk barefoot than with shoes, especially on that pebbled cement. Without the platform of a shoe under them, they were liable to fold up under my feet. I held on to the rail at the steps and stuck one of my toes in the water. It was even colder than I'd expected. I looked at Candy and winced.

"Nobody's making you do this," she said. "You'll still be a hero as far as I'm concerned."

"Fuck off," I said.

She laughed.

I walked around to the ladder by the deep end. I began to get goose bumps just thinking about the cold. I held on to the ladder and began to rock back and forth. With a final thought of *to hell with it*, I tried to leap out. My foot might as well have slipped, as I didn't leap at all, but instantly became horizontal and hit the water with a loud smack. Before the frigid shock could register, I knew something was wrong. The stroke had taken away my ability to hold my breath underwater. My soft palate, in the back of my throat, was so weak (it's still quite weak), it couldn't keep water from flooding in through my nose. My body turned rigid and started to sink. The water stung as it came flooding into my throat, while I floundered at the surface gasping for air and swallowing what seemed to be half of the pool. I never got scared, though. I never had time. Before fear could come into play, Candy had jumped into the water with her jeans and tennis shoes on, grabbed my shirt, and was paddling us both to the shallow end.

"You okay?" she said breathlessly when we could stand up. The soaked sleeves of her sweatshirt were draped over her hands.

I nodded and coughed some more. "Jesus," I said. "I would've been fine." At the time I may have believed this, though it's obvious in hindsight I would have drowned.

That morning Candy had told me she wanted us to drink a beer together before she left. I knew she no longer wanted to, but we ceremonially sat at the kitchen table and toasted anyway. Her clothes weren't dripping any longer—she hadn't wanted to put them in the dryer for some reason—but she was still shivering. She tried to be serious and say that, no kidding, I really was a hero. She could never have imagined this day. I thanked her, and she left before she finished her beer. I drank the rest of mine in silence. Then I went to the bathroom and threw it back up.

A day came, a few months later, when my parents said it was time to let Candy go. I was finished with outpatient therapy, so I no longer needed the rides. And at home I needed less and less caretaking. Not that I was fully recovered, but I could do things for myself. I had progressed, or adapted, enough to bathe and dress myself at least. I was ready for her to go, too. As much as she helped me, she was in the way of my independence.

On the afternoon before what was supposed to be her last day, she said she'd see me tomorrow, but even in the moment something told me that I wouldn't see her. Neither of us needed a "last day." She wanted to end on a good note. Before me, everyone she'd worked with had been elderly and was not going to get any better. When the person either moved into a nursing home or died, Candy moved on. She'd said before that she might give up being a sitter after me. As strange as it sounded, she really couldn't stand hospitals. She didn't know what she would do next.

Candy had grown up in Birmingham during the height of the civil rights struggle. She remembered riding through downtown as a little girl and having to lie on the floor of the car. She'd given birth to a son at eighteen, out of wedlock, and moved to Alaska, where the boy's father left her. She went through a string of relationships before meeting the man she was married to when I met her, an old high school boyfriend who'd adopted her son. She saw all things as temporary, the way I'd come to see them. Both of us viewed an emotional, stock-taking goodbye as unnecessary and insincere. We said we'd keep in touch.

19

—

Dewin tells me that when I first came to him, I used to "snort" when I tried to sing. That was the word he used. My voice would catch, and a sort of snorting would come out. I can't remember the sound, but I trust his memory. If I thought I could stand listening to it, I'd go back through the years of CDs of our lessons until I heard it. He remembers that when we started working together and needed to communicate between lessons, I'd get someone else to call for me, because my voice wasn't intelligible. I'd forgotten that, too. He says he knew I was making progress when he called my phone one day and could understand my words on the greeting. He says he notices that when I make the right sound with my mouth, my body straightens. Untwists. The tongue is a "rudder," he says. Set it right, and the body will fall into line. He says he can actually watch this happen with me, watch the shoulder I tend to hitch start settling into place, and the one I tend to let drop rise, until they're level. The vowels I was making had more symmetry than my damaged body.

"I know that the voice will find a way, if you can get a sound out, to be as symmetrical as possible. I don't know the extent to which you lost the muscles to control what happens in that process. I'm not sure how much the vowels have taught other parts of your brain to hold that part of your throat open, and how much we just reanimated what was already there. I think there's probably a combination of things going on, that you're learning new neuronal pathways to get to what you need."

I said that the lack of control was why the speech person I eventually saw dismissed me as a lost cause.

"Well, he was wrong," he said. "Or maybe what he was right about was that you had lost the control, but what he was wrong about was your ability to work around the problem. I think the body's ability to grow toward solving its problems, the brain's problems, and the physics of those vowel sounds, and the acoustics, were kind of reaching toward each other to figure it out. It's been slow, but hey, it's been a steady ascent."

One of the things that makes Dewin a good teacher for someone like me is all the work he's done with boys' choirs, helping adolescents whose voices were changing. He explained to me that the reason teenage boys' voices crack like that has to do with the change in their body mass. They're getting heavier, and as a result their body is becoming a different instrument. It's changing from a viola to a cello, or from a cello to a bass, but there's a period where they're in between, and all that new muscle mass is untrained, it's soft. That's when you get the cracking between octaves. During that period, Dewin said, these boys would do a lot of the same things with their bodies I was doing, trying to build a "leverage device." Only I was starting from much farther back. They were trying to strengthen their voices. I was trying "to relearn, as an adult, this elegant relationship of physics that we learn as infants."

Still, all that experience made him a good empathizer. He can look at a certain outward gesture and know immediately what inner phenomenon, what contortion of invisible muscles, has produced it. Sometimes he'll have me sing while holding a plastic knife in my teeth, to keep me from trying to help the sound with my lips. He told me this is akin to how Demosthenes, the Greek statesman and orator, taught his students 2,400 years ago. He'd have them put pebbles in their mouths to speak around. There are moments, in Dewin's studio, when I feel like a human sculpture he's working on, slowly, without ever laying a hand or a hammer on me. He's telepathically changing the configuration of the musculature in my body. He does this for all his students, but with me it's more visible. Seven years in, people understand me at dinner parties (not that I go to many). I have developed a falsetto.

20

Looking back, the path to now, to sitting at this desk and writing, seems so unarbitrary that it's almost impossible to deny the work of an outside hand. This is a comfort at times, enough to keep me grounded. But it also requires a perspective that lies outside of the action. Fate, so called, only works in retrospect. You can't experience it and understand it at the same time. The notion of fate appears only when we consider ourselves as unified consciousnesses moving through time, but such an identity is merely a role—or at least that's how I've come to see it.

Before the wreck, I'd never done much writing. I liked reading, and occasionally I would jot down some thoughts, but nothing continuous, just isolated impressions. I do remember, even in those moments, feeling the pleasure that could come from playing with language and finding the right words. After the wreck and stroke, it was one of the few pleasures available to me, so I began to seek it out. As a way to validate my time, at first, and then gradually, as a way to survive. For me it has been a healing obsession.

The rest of college—when I finally went back, a year and a half after the stroke—was eye-opening and miserable. In all my planning and hard physical work to return, in all my wondering about how I would be received, I'd forgotten to consider that everyone else on campus would have moved on. No one was waiting for me like I'd expected. Nor had I imagined that my former friends might be apprehensive about my return. I have a journal entry from my first months that sums up what I felt fairly well.

12/2/94

When I first started writing after the stroke (when I could remember what "normal" felt like), a friend said, "At least you know you've been through the toughest part of your life." Well that was wrong; not being included in my friends' activities, for whatever the reason, is just as hard or harder than the issue of survival. I guess I'd envisioned some sort of praise, but instead, people tend to make me feel like I've done something wrong. I shouldn't expect everyone to be so "shit happens" philosophical about this as me. Nonetheless, I'm still human, so if I can get past this (and it's happening to me), why is it so hard for other people? It's trying, being inundated with people who don't think for themselves, and not having anyone to identify with. The only reason this hell is bearable is because of my ability to laugh. I still (with no logical basis) can't help but think something good has got to come out of this. It's still as unbelievable as ever.

One day, the dean of students invited me to lunch, at a place right across the street from my dorm. It was a humid, sunny day, and I almost felt good. I tried to be as casual as I could walking in with the dean. He was a sharp, laid-back, relatively young guy who taught some classes and interacted with the students all the time, but he was still an authority figure. After the wreck he'd driven my parents and my sister, who threw up in his car, down the back way to the hospital in Chattanooga.

"How about your classes?" he asked after we'd ordered. "Everything going okay there?"

I told him it was. "I'm gonna like Ethics, I think."

He carried our tray to a table in the window.

"Let me know if I can do anything," he said.

In the early part of the century a girl from Sewanee had drowned while swimming in Lake Cheston. Since then her parents had made it one of the college's traditions that you had to swim across the lake to graduate. I'd been fretting about this ever since discovering I could no longer swim. I didn't want to be excluded, though, and I was ready to die not to be. Maybe I could float on my back. Was there a time limit?

Once he'd figured out what I was talking about, he started smiling. "You don't have to worry about that," he said. "We quit that a couple of years ago."

A group of guys with black streaks on their faces and chests came running in, chanting something I couldn't understand. Their shirts were stuffed in their back pockets, and each held close to the person in front of him. They tried to hide their faces as they shuffled around a table where a guy and two girls were sitting. Their chanting changed. The guy at the table smiled bashfully and stood up. They picked him up over their heads and carried him out just as they'd come in. It was fraternity rush week.

The dean shook his head and laughed. "Y'all don't do that, do you?"

"Y'all?"

"The Phis."

"Oh, God," I said. "I'm not having any part in that shi . . . in that, anymore."

"No?" he said, raising his eyebrows. "It could be good for you. You know, a way to get back into campus life."

"Maybe." I pretended to think about it. "I don't know." But I did know. I wasn't about to associate myself with a bunch of predominantly unknown party guys for whom I would likely become something like a mascot.

"Sometimes," I said, "I wish all of my brain had been affected. So I wouldn't know. Most of the things I've learned from what I've been through, I'd rather not know."

The dean smiled apologetically. He then put both of

his elbows on the table like he was going to lean forward and tell me a secret. "But you know," he said. "You do."

Will and I quickly began to get on each other's nerves. I had been given the role of his silent sidekick—and by extension, his little brother. He had been relegated to the role of my interpreter. Neither of us liked it. He had a girlfriend, so his presence was never as constant as I would have liked, though when he was there, we fought. I wanted a girlfriend, too. But I wasn't about to ask anyone out. I started pointing out Will's faults instead: he drank too much, he smoked too much, his impatience was going to kill him. He began calling me the Critic. "What do you do?" he said. "Not shit. You sit around here feeling sorry for yourself and you take it out on me."

I got out and started taking walks. I began walking to the Cross, a sixty-foot memorial out on a bluff with a dramatic view of the valley below, which was down the street from our dorm. It was dedicated to Sewanee students who'd fought in World War I. The distance there and back was only a little more than a mile. I got to know every tilt of the road and imperfection in the pavement, but on one of the first mornings, I'd gotten to where the woods began, right after the soccer field, when I heard footsteps coming up behind me. The frost on the lawns hadn't begun to evaporate and the trees still hid the sun. I turned around to see a girl jogging in gray sweatpants and new turquoise running shoes.

"Hi," she said breathlessly as she slowed her arms to a

stop. She leaned forward and put her hands on her knees. "My name's Anna." She extended her hand. "I've seen you around but I haven't had a chance to introduce myself."

I told her I was Will Byars's brother.

She had long, wispy blond hair, dark, partially closed eyes, and porcelain skin with veins pulsating in her temples. She nodded and smiled, then looked confused. She didn't know Will. Then she said she was a sophomore, and I told her that technically I was, too. This led into my history, which I tried to downplay as much as I could, emphasizing "brain stem" stroke, as if anyone would know this was the kind that didn't affect cognition.

Three or four days later, I walked to the Cross again. This time I didn't get started until the late afternoon. As I started down the sidewalk, I saw a group of four or five girls headed my way. They saw me, too, and turned in toward each other as we passed, to avoid noticing me. I tensed up and tried to look as harmless as possible. I saw Anna in the back of the group. We made eye contact, and I smiled. Then she dropped her eyes and moved up beside the girl in front of her, causing a rush of disbelief and shame that made me replay the incident for weeks.

I did make a new friend, though, a Chinese woman named Nai-Chian. She was running a restaurant in town, the City Café, one of the few local places not owned by the school. It was a quiet, sit-down place that didn't serve alcohol and had flower arrangements on the tables. It was the type of place you'd take your grandmother if she came to visit you. I used to go in the mornings for the blueberry-

and-banana pancakes, and sometimes for the spicy chicken and rice at lunch. Nai-Chian would quietly pick up the chopsticks from my table and set down a spoon for me to eat the rice with. She and I started talking one day when business was slow. She didn't say it, but I could tell she felt like an outsider as much as I did. This became our unspoken bond, and the basis of our friendship—but that was all it was. Her husband, a burly local who worked for the school's physical plant, silently eyed me with suspicion.

I couldn't tell how old she was. She had close-cropped, pageboy black hair, was short and in good shape. She taught a tai chi class every morning that met in the park. She didn't look any older than thirty-five, but may have been fifty-five. She was an accomplished seamstress, too. Later, for my birthday, she knitted me a pillow with my Chinese zodiac sign on it. The ox.

Writing absorbed my attention more and more. A well-known poet who taught at the school, Wyatt Prunty, was offering an independent study in short fiction. He agreed to let me in even though I'd recently declared philosophy as my major—a small act of kindness that's had a major effect on my life. I spent days holed up, trying out stories, but I couldn't get one to work at first. When I finally did, in an admittedly short amount of time, I felt something akin to security. I was able to escape myself and trust myself at the same time. Every word felt both inevitable and full of potential. When that story was later accepted for publication in the school literary magazine, I remember I felt almost as good seeing it in print as when I'd finished it and knew I had something. No longer was I simply that guy who left and came back; I was a writer. The looks of confusion I got down at the bar from a group of girls I didn't know, as if they now had to recalibrate their knowledge about me, were exhilarating. Everything would continue to flow from now on.

Then I tried to write another story. It didn't happen. Then another. And another. I was distraught. The more I learned about the mechanics of writing, the more my stories seemed lifeless. There wasn't any depth to them, no risk involved. They were just clever cuts into the surface, and sometimes not even that. Reason told me, "Why mess around and possibly fuck up your underlying sense of well-being? Go somewhere less personally relevant, less sincere." Looking for any shortcut to hard work and serious consideration, I tried to locate the problem everywhere but within me. And that "me" seemed to be getting more and more contained as time went by. At times, frustrated, I experienced feelings reminiscent of when I'd been locked in, when I hadn't been able to move or speak. But then I'd had only one option, whereas with stories, multiple options always seemed to exist.

One night I woke up at two o'clock and couldn't go back to sleep. I threw off the covers. It was cold but I didn't care. I marched to the study and wrote—not typed but wrote longhand—a letter to Eleanor, saying we needed to get together. I told her it was my fault we hadn't before, I was just scared. But I wasn't going to sit and watch our relationship dwindle to insignificance, which I could tell was already starting. I included my phone number and asked her to call me when she got the letter. A sense of determination and happiness kept me up the rest of the night. I mailed it as soon as the campus post office opened the following morning. But after two weeks went by without a response, my hope sank into ambivalence. What had I been thinking? I was oddly relieved when eventually the letter came back, Return to Sender: Change of Address Unknown.

21

When I came home one Friday during my last semester, I think, I saw Candy's car parked in our driveway. I couldn't help smiling. It had been almost a year since I'd seen her—an afternoon when I'd driven out to her house in Forestdale, a small community about half an hour from Birmingham. The trip had been to celebrate getting my driver's license back. Walking to the door now, I wondered what her visit was about.

I couldn't see her through the door glass at first. When I walked into the kitchen she was down to my left with her back facing me. Her hair was tied up in a bandana, and she was bent forward as she pushed a mop back and forth across the floor. A bucket of dark, soapy water sat next to her.

"Hey," I said as the door shut behind me.

She cupped both hands over the end of the mop and straightened up. "All right," she said, slightly out of breath. "How's it goin', man?"

"Did you spill something?" My stomach started to sink.

"Aw, no." She looked at the mop. "Check this out, Mrs. B. asked me to clean y'all's house."

I chuckled. "What did you tell her?"

"I can't on Mondays, Tuesdays, or Thursdays, but any other day will work. Why?"

This wasn't happening. How could she do this? I suppose I'd thought we were in this together somehow. But apparently she was perfectly happy to go from being the keeper of my mother's retarded son to being her cleaning girl.

"What?" Candy said, like I'd accused her of something. Probably she thought I was going to be happy.

Quickly I realized I was being a spoiled shithead. She and I both knew that my mother would pay her well, better than she could get most anywhere else. She could see, though, that I was upset.

"I didn't know your other job was just part-time," I said.

"Both of my other jobs are part-time."

I didn't reply. I gathered up my books and hobbled back to my room, feeling ashamed and uneasy. We didn't talk any more before Candy left that day. She seemed to be avoiding me as much as I was her. But when I saw her again a few weeks later, it was like nothing had ever happened. She continued to clean the house for a year or so before she said she was moving back to Alaska. A little while after that, however, my sister swore she saw Candy in a yellow station wagon with the logo of a professional maid service on the side.

22

After graduating, I had no idea what I was going to do. Lots of college graduates say that, but I truly had no idea, about what I wanted to do or even what my options were. I only knew what I didn't want to do: anything to do with stagnation. My parents seemed content with my doing nothing. I'd already triumphed in their eyes, for which I'm thankful now but at the time I took as yet another uncomfortable indicator. The lack of expectation—from anyone—gave me some sense of freedom. But that didn't last long.

When I was in this state, my first disability check came. I can't really blame my father for signing me up for benefits. For once I was overly qualified for something. But I did resent it, and I again became distraught in an almost out-of-body way. Was this really happening? It seemed as if the door to the future, any future, was now shut and dead-bolted behind me. I felt trapped.

Mainly to breathe, but also to be able to do things for myself without my parents jumping all over me, I decided to move to our family's lake cabin two hours south of Birmingham and try to write about everything that had happened. I knew there was more to the story than just the facts of what had happened to me. I decided that I should turn it into a novel. I can remember setting up my computer on one end of the kitchen table and self-consciously thinking, "It starts here." I was sure the final product would somehow save me. From what exactly, I didn't know. All I needed to do was write it.

I worked on it diligently for months, trying various approaches to avoid presenting myself as someone who'd simply and sentimentally beaten the odds. I'd written my senior philosophy paper on Aristotle's use of *katharsis* in the Poetics, but that approach—turning my story into a tragedy—seemed too confining. But the story refused to be contained. Like before, I was living it while I was trying to write about it. Trying to make graduating from college the end, when I didn't even walk to receive my diploma, just felt too much like an after-school special. I'm thankful, as much as I wanted otherwise, that I was able to step out of the way.

Shortly after I moved into the lake house, I saw a fox out on the deck one night. We'd had the house since I was in the fifth grade, and I'd seen plenty of wild animals around there through the years, but I'd never seen a fox, not up close like that. Maybe it thought no one was there. Usually that was the case. I thought that by switching on the floodlights, I could make it leave. I was wrong. Nor did it run off when I opened the door. It tried, but the deck sat about fifteen feet off the ground, and the only way off (besides jumping) was the set of stairs it must have taken up, and I was standing by those. It scrabbled to two different corners before realizing it would have to confront my presence. Something about its skittishness and size made me completely unafraid.

I thought about cutting the lights again, because I knew how scared it must be, but instead of walking over to the switch, I just stepped back inside the screen door and gave it a chance to get away. Finally it walked back to the top of the steps. But it didn't descend. It stood there.

Once the animal was back under the light, I realized that it wasn't what I'd thought. Everything about it looked exactly like a fox, even its size, except it didn't have a long, bushy tail. The one it did have was only about a foot long. I'd heard of other wild-domestic hybrids—especially of wolves and coyotes—and I wondered if that's what this thing was. It had no collar. It just looked wild, and it definitely acted wild. I guessed that it hadn't run off because it was starving. There was a grill on the deck that it may have smelled. It had a lean snout and body, and what looked like mange or some other skin disease, but it didn't appear emaciated. Whatever it was, it wasn't going anywhere.

I went inside and found some bread, then walked back out and set it down. After I stepped back, the creature immediately crept up and sniffed, but didn't eat. It looked up at me instead. I didn't know what it wanted, and I wasn't about to touch it. After we'd stared at each other for a few more seconds, I went back inside and cut the lights.

The next morning the bread was gone, but I didn't see the fox-dog. I went outside and walked around the cabin. There was no sign. I even called out, "Hey!" but got back only silence. Romantic visions of taming a wild animal—validating my existence and perfecting the *Walden*-like qualities of it—vanished with strangely little regret, considering the enthusiasm with which they'd formed.

I left to go walking that afternoon, and before I'd even reached the base of the big hill that the cabin sat on, I turned around and found that she—I could clearly see now that she was a girl, her tail was up—was following me. Over the next two weeks, she was always there, whenever I went outside, waiting for me to give her something to eat. I wasn't fully committed yet, toward claiming her as mine—I hadn't named her—but I was starting to suspect that she wasn't going anywhere.

One morning I looked out the kitchen window and saw her running along the beach that forms every winter when the water level drops. A rust-colored animal was chasing her, just a blur. I hurried outside, hoping the pursuer would see me and run off. But they were just playing. They darted among the sand and rocks, and neither was trying that hard to catch or get caught. Both noticed me at the same time and stopped in their tracks. It was as if I'd caught them at something they knew they shouldn't be doing. I started to laugh. The fox-dog, with a lowered back, began creeping toward me and the other reluctantly followed. I could see as it walked that it was undeniably a dog, a bigger fluffy dog, mainly chow, with a tail that curled back over its body. It wasn't wearing a collar either, but it clearly was, or had been, someone's pet. It carried itself like an animal used to responding to commands.

I went back inside, hoping it would eventually get bored and go on its way. I didn't want to have to take care of another animal. It was only then that I realized I'd already resigned myself to taking care of the fox-dog for her brief life. For some reason I was sure that it would be brief. She was already full-grown. How much longer could she have?

I didn't throw out any scraps that day for her food, because I didn't want the chow to take it and get any ideas.

When I set out to go walking the next morning, only the fox-dog came out from under the cabin to join me. I walked for about an hour, to a spot little more than a mile from the cabin, where my road intersected with another. I was strolling along, thinking how fortunate I was to have escaped having another mouth to feed, when the chow came crashing out of the woods like he was late for an appointment.

After days of failed efforts to get rid of him—which included cutting off the food supply and forcibly relocating him to a gated community five miles away—I decided he, too, had earned his keep. I named the two immediately, before I had time to think about it. Clinging maybe to a vestige of my original romantic vision for the cabin, I named them Daisy and Jay, after the lovers in *The Great Gatsby*. That night I put out two bowls of food.

A few months later, after a bloody fight over food, I took them to the local vet to get checked out. That's when I discovered my error. Because everything about Jay said male, I never thought to check under all that fur. It turned out, however, that he was a she. She picked fights with everything, no matter its size, and she usually won. I saw her back down from another dog only once—a much bigger pound dog—that she then became friends with so they could be bullies together. She peed with a raised leg, too, which I found out was because one of her back legs was shorter than the other one. And if any other animal wandered onto my property, she, followed by Daisy, promptly ran it off—or if it were an unsuspecting rabbit, raccoon, or armadillo, they would kill it.

Once I was in the kitchen and saw Daisy through the window, and for a second I thought she'd had a stroke. She was standing, but otherwise seemed to have become catatonic. Walking out, I looked at the tree she was facing, and saw a cat trapped halfway up it. Daisy had the focused, dispassionate gaze of a predator on the Serengeti, as if she'd become one half of an equation that already had an answer. The cat must have sensed this, too, because it started crying. Daisy didn't blink, nor did she respond in the slightest to my commands to leave it alone. I finally had to go back inside and get a leash to pull her away. She was transformed. For a second I thought she might even attack me.

It took only a little while before the dogs figured out that, although I may be a pushover in some areas, I'm also lazy enough not to bother with the initiative needed for discipline. After a few times waiting around while the dogs were off in the woods, when I was ready to go to Birmingham, I started leaving them. They looked hurt and betrayed when I returned, as if I'd broken a rule, but they caught on quick. At first they'd looked to me for direction in all circumstances. When they saw it wasn't coming, they learned to think for themselves. We became something like a team, belonging to one another, however unwittingly. No matter where we were, in what house or what town, Daisy slept in the bed next to me, and Jay on the threshold of the door to that room.

23

Six months into my stay at the lake, I had a complete draft of my "novel." I knew it didn't work. Parts did, but basically, nothing held it together. It wasn't a story so much as an account. I decided I needed to become a better writer before trying again. I gave away one of the beds in the guest bedroom, put a prefabricated desk in there, and began to read and write in greater earnest, meaning that was pretty much all I did. My reading mainly consisted of short stories and novels, since that's what I was trying to write. I have a strong memory of reading an early translation of *Anna Karenina* by candlelight while drenched in a filmy sweat because the power had gone out again. It's one of the few objective images I have of myself from that period. I had stopped imagining myself as much, or picturing myself from the outside. I did go up to Birmingham every once in a while, to get my "social fix," but going out on the town involved subjecting myself to a sea of first impressions that remained most people's only impression.

My stories were mostly weak imitations of writing I liked, but I was prolific, and I showed them to whoever would read them, offering them as some kind of proof. My only truly loyal reader was my grandmother, who read each one multiple times. After my grandfather's death, when I was in high school, she'd moved to a ground-floor apartment that had its own roof—part of a complex that my parents had lived in as newlyweds. O'mama began spending more and more of her time reading. She'd always been an avid reader and had written some reviews when she was younger, but as her friends began dying off, reading filled a void. She would check out ten books a week from the library, and when her eyesight began fading, if she couldn't find a large-print edition of a book she wanted to read, she'd scan the pages with a magnifying glass.

I trusted her opinion of my work. O'mama's aunt and namesake, Blanche Colton Williams, had been the inaugural editor of the O. Henry Memorial Awards in 1918. Until Oprah Winfrey came along, she was (according to O'mama) the best-known person to come out of Kosciusko, Mississippi. O'mama also had a first cousin, Wirt Williams, who moved to L.A. after World War II and became a successful novelist.

I went over to her apartment to read and write on the

afternoons I was in town. She would take her two fingers of bourbon and Coca-Cola into the closet of a den to watch *Judge Judy* while I sat at the dining room table and lost track of time. She would occasionally come out for more fingers and to report on the latest case, always idiotic and easily simplified by Judy, and eventually she'd sit down to discuss my latest story. She didn't give a comprehensive critique of them like a writing professor would have done, but she knew if a story didn't work. "It fits together" was about as detailed as she got. But she could tell when my writing started to get tighter, after I'd given up the novel and started writing short fiction again. I believed her because I thought so, too.

One of my first attempts was about an old lady with a Pomeranian and a sense of entitlement who's become addicted to painkillers after losing her husband. I'd been reluctant to show it to her, because it was clearly based on her—at one point detailing exactly an argument she'd had with her sister—but she walked out to the dining room that day shaking the rolled-up pages and said, "Oh, Clay, one of your best. You're definitely on your way."

"I thought you might get mad."

She smiled. "Mad? Why? I don't have a dog."

I didn't point out all the other similarities, but I don't think she would have cared anyway. Writing, my writing specifically, existed on a different plane from the one she lived on. It couldn't touch her, and at the same time she was protective of it. I knew that her enthusiasm wasn't just grandmotherly cheerleading, because she'd let me know if she didn't think a story worked, usually by immediately asking about another one she thought did. She tried to get me to submit them for publication, and some I did, but after getting rejected by most of the big names, I moved on to another story.

"I just wish Bibs was still around," she said, talking about her aunt. Blanche would have given better advice.

The only other person who took an interest in my writing during the months I spent at the cabin—not that many people got close enough to take an interest—was a man named Jack. He never read anything I wrote, but he took an interest in the sheer fact that I was writing. He and my father had lived together after college. He'd grown up in a small town just a few miles away from where the cabin stood. Like my father, Jack could and would talk to anyone, always establishing a historical context for the relationship. When meeting one of my friends, sooner or later he'd come around to the question, "Who are your people?" He seemed like a character straight out of a Peter Taylor story, or like Taylor himself, on one level an upper-middle-class, country-club-attending Southern gentleman, but with so many levels to his character, only a fool would take him for one-dimensional. He easily could have taught history, both of the American South and of Saudi Arabia, where he'd lived for most of his adult life. He was the perfect friend to have at the lake, because he knew everyone and everyone knew him. Given that I was an aspiring writer, he took it as his duty to show me everything in the immediate area that might be culturally of interest. Once we went to a Baptist tent revival at a country church. We got a behind-the-scenes tour at Horseshoe Bend National Military Park, where Jack had once been a ranger. Another time we met with the commandant of a nearby military school where Jack was a donor. He told us that most of the students were problem kids who'd been kicked out of other places, but that about 35 percent were there willingly.

"No offense," I said, "but why would anyone come here willingly?" The high, enclosing fence and the complete absence of a smile on every uniformed cadet we saw looked like punishment to me.

He paused for effect and announced, "Struck-shah."

Jack kept in shape with a personal trainer, who was also the owner of a gym in town. I started going there, as well—not to the elite, private room Jack went to with his trainer, but the main floor. People stared at first, but after a while I became a familiar sight, since I went there so much. I didn't mind. It didn't mean they talked to me, but at least they acknowledged me.

I'd never been very rigorous when it came to working out, but I became religious about making time. As with the voice lessons, I saw results instantly, especially after Jack's trainer gave me an individualized set of exercises. My body still had very little natural tension or balance in it. My default position was like that of a collapsed marionette—one side weakened, the other spastic. Nothing was holding me up. Staying vertical involved a conscious exertion of strength, and I had to center my weight over my feet. So as my muscles developed, my posture and my stability improved dramatically. I no longer had to go around feeling like I might bust my ass every second.

24

When Will and I were in high school, the Home Depot came to Birmingham. Its aisled warehouses and ubiquitous customer service have since become a model for many other chains, but it was somewhat revolutionary at the time. One weekend my father went to one in a shopping center near our house, whether just to browse or for something specific, I don't know. As he was walking back to his car in the fairly crowded lot, a man appeared beside him and started chatting. My father returned the small talk. (He was not only a master of small talk, he could cut people off just as quickly. "Well, good enough.") Once they reached his car, the man, obviously realizing his plan wasn't working out as smoothly as envisioned, reached into my father's inside jacket pocket as he was climbing behind the wheel and took his wallet. From my father's recounting of the incident, I don't know how the man could have thought this would be taken as just an accidental brush, but apparently he did. My father hadn't seen the man take it, but he felt it leave his pocket. Nevertheless, he patted his chest and said, "You son of a bitch, you just took my wallet."

The man said, "Sir, I don't know what you're talking about." My father said he just had it next to his glasses and now it's not there. Then the man said, "You're welcome to frisk me if you don't believe me." He knew then he was part of a scam. The man had passed the wallet off to someone else walking by at just the right moment that my father hadn't noticed, but my father frisked him anyway. He of course didn't find it. The man said he must have dropped it on the floor and said he would go check himself. My father followed him back inside, but of course it wasn't there either. The man even offered to take his card and call him if it turned up.

I don't know if the man just expected him to go back to his car and curse his bad luck before going home to cancel his credit cards, but my father went back to his car and moved it until he was out of sight. Then he sat there waiting for three and a half hours. My mother finally called his cell phone to check on him. When the man finally came out, he looked around before walking to a car in the lot next door. My father sped over and blocked him in while he began to write down the license plate number. As he was doing this, the man jumped out of his car and came back to my father's. My father admitted this next part was stupid, and he could easily have been shot. The man said something he had to roll down his window to hear. He was asking my father what he thought he was doing. When my father told him he was writing down his tag number, the man said, "I'm sorry about your wallet, sir, but you can't do that. You're violating my civil liberties."

My father said, "I suggest you watch me," and rolled up his window.

By the time he returned home, the local Wal-Mart had called, and his wallet, without missing a thing, had been found on the floor there. He called the police nevertheless.

In the early fall of 2006, my father fell ill. His stubbornness had helped get him to where he was in life, but as he admitted himself, it could blind him. Stubbornness kept him from going to the doctor before he and my mother left on a trip for Italy. He'd sold his company, so he and my mother began traveling a good bit, to be able to deal with the leisure. He'd been complaining of stomach pains, to the point of almost getting himself checked out. He said after the trip that he knew he shouldn't have gone, but I understand why he did. Immediately on returning, after complaining to us about all the hills and stairs in Italy, he checked himself into the hospital. Two days and a battery of negative tests later, he was released. His pains didn't stop, however, so he went to see his internist, who couldn't find anything either, but urged my father to check himself back into the hospital.

When I got into town that night, my mother was just leaving to take him his toothbrush and a change of clothes. His stay was indefinite, at least until they found out why his stomach hurt. We were in the kitchen, and I told my mother not to worry about my dinner, I would just heat up some leftovers. Then I said, "The fatalistic way Dad's handling all this isn't going to help him. You even said yourself he's sure he has cancer. I told him he hasn't always been like this. He's basically being a pitiful, passive patient."

My mother glared at me in disbelief. "But Clay, he's sixty-seven years old."

"I know. All I'm saying is that he's one of the main reasons I've been able to recover at all. He hasn't always been this mentally pitiful. He's just waiting to die."

She got that caged-animal look in her eye. I wasn't getting my viewpoint across, and she was getting angry. "But he's your father," she said.

"That's not . . ."

"You could have a little compassion, you schmuck!"

I don't remember hearing the phone ring, but I was awoken at two o'clock the next morning and heard her talking on the phone across the hall. It was one of my father's nurses. My mother said, "Oh, my God!" He'd started throwing up blood, and they were taking him to the ICU. He was still lucid enough to have the nurse call home. I walked in to find my mother frantically getting dressed. My sister was on the way to pick her up. They would call and let me know what was going on as soon as they knew themselves. "Don't worry," my mother added, opening her umbrella by the front door and stepping out into the pouring night, "it's all under control."

We learned that polio can cause problems later in life for people who've had the disease when they were young. My father had always been in remarkably good health, apart from being overweight, and neither his family nor my mother's had any history of cancer. Were his years catching up to him?

They gave him an emergency endoscopy that night, hoping to find the source of his pain. The doctor had to put him to sleep for this, but my mother wanted Will and me to see him first, in case he didn't wake up. Her cell phone went straight to voice mail when I called to tell her to stop being so theatrical, and not to wait on us. Time was obviously of the essence. I called again and got the same result. I felt like I was back in the hospital, having another needless test that no one had ordered.

It turned out that my father's liver was failing. It had been for a long time. The diagnosis, cirrhosis, made me assume that alcohol had played a part, but as it turned out, this wasn't the case. My father did drink, but he wasn't an alcoholic. His unchecked diet and the curvature of his spine were factors, the doctors said.

His relief at not having cancer was short-lived. He needed a new liver, and soon. He began to turn yellow— not yellowish, but comical, face-paint yellow. They put him on a quarantined ward. Before entering, we had to put on gowns and masks and scrub up with antibacterial soap. A friend of ours, Will's best friend from elementary school, was doing a residency in the hospital at the time. He visited my father every day of the two weeks he was there. He told us later that if a new liver hadn't arrived when it did, my father would surely have died. "You don't think he could have made it another day?" I asked. He responded, "I don't think he could have made it more than a few hours."

The color of my father's face went back to normal almost immediately after the transplant, but he remained certain that he was dying. Yet there was none of the expected fear in his eyes, of the kind that might prompt him to act, either to end it or to get better. We gathered around the bed, and he began writing out what he wanted to say. His throat being intubated for so long had left him unable, or too weak, to speak. Then he got tired and had me go through the alphabet letter by letter, while he spelled out his thoughts. He wanted to know the date. He wanted to say that his nurse was a bitch. That his back was hurting. As we were leaving, he tried to tell my mother something, which couldn't have been that important, because he didn't want to spell it out. He wanted to make us guess. He made a halfhearted effort to pantomime his thoughts, at one point folding his hands over his chest. When none of us could figure out what he was trying to say, he fell back on the pillow and shook his head in disgust, like we'd failed him.

I don't think he ever really gave the transplant a chance to take. He'd decided he didn't want to live anymore. Yet he was afraid to die. I didn't blame him—neither for the fear nor for no longer wanting to live. There was something intuitive between us. We understood each other, and he now trusted me. At the same time, I couldn't escape mixed feelings for having gained it this way. It had required his complete dependence on someone he knew could relate, whereas his instinct was to act for me.

The house became a theater of blame. For my mother and sister, it all came down to something one of the doctors was doing wrong. Will had two little girls by that time, and it was easiest for me to be involved. Once I drove downtown in the middle of the night, after my father had called home raging in frustration, demanding his street clothes. I arrived only to find him asleep. He called on Christmas morning to tell the family that it had been a good run. He ended up deciding he'd been having a nervous breakdown, and his doctors even sent the psychologist on staff to see him. I walked into his room while she was there, but he wanted to tell her all about me instead of discussing what was going on with him. She rolled her eyes after a while, and he looked at me and smiled before continuing. I explained to him that he could leave as soon as he was able to sit in a wheelchair for ten minutes. "But I can't," he said. "I can't."

"How do you know if you don't try?" I said.

It was like a fog moved in. He looked straight ahead, then he made his eyes roll back in his head, as if to blot out what was happening.

He died a few weeks later, after a prolonged refusal to eat. A machine was the only thing that kept his heart beating. His final moments were appropriately theatrical. A minister friend of his was there. We gathered around his bed in the ICU as they unplugged him, which was surreal because he was conscious, although intubated and groggy, as if he'd just woken up from a dream. His eyes were open. The doctor had said it would be just a matter of seconds before he flatlined, once he came off the cardiopulmonary pump, but he was lucid enough and had time to gesture first. He moved his hand. The minister beckoned us all to huddle up.

25

One day a few months later, after I'd moved from the lake to Shelby, I went to lunch with Caldwell's father, who I still saw fairly regularly. He wondered if I had ever considered teaching, at which I just laughed. He said he could really tell a difference in my voice and thought I could do it if I wanted. Then he told me about this experimental school downtown, where inner-city kids, most from single-parent families, from all over the area applied as a first step on their way to college—the school only went through the eighth grade. Charter schools hadn't yet come to Alabama, but that's essentially what this was. He had donated some money to the school, but wasn't involved otherwise. He said he'd love to take me to go meet the principal if this was something I might want. I could tell he had put some thought into this, so I said sure. The man we met with was the interim principal—the acting principal had stepped down the week before—and was an ex–army officer. Caldwell's father explained what he had in mind, that I teach or tutor some of the older kids in creative writing and help them with their papers. The principal agreed to it before Caldwell's father even finished, which automatically made me suspicious, but then we met with the volunteer coordinator and I felt better. (I couldn't remember the last time I'd had to fill out a background check, either.)

Right away, I realized I'd severely underestimated these kids. Even though I later discovered that the two girls I first taught were the best writers in the school, there was none of the lively discussion that I'd envisioned. This was beginning creative writing, for which they both had an intuitive feeling, but which they couldn't have talked about and I wasn't prepared to teach, and I was expected to talk the entire time. I didn't know what I was going to do. Not long after, I happened upon an exercise guide for college graduates that was divided up, loosely, by the different parts of a story. It saved me. I had to tailor some of the exercises for seventh- and eighth-grade level, but except for the ones dealing with sex, they all more or less worked. Plus, I couldn't give homework, so this seemed perfect. This was creative writing, after all. They would learn by doing it. I later found other exercises, as well as ones for poetry, and came up with some on my own, but that became the format—making them think for themselves in a framed setting—from then on. The biggest group I had was eight students, sometimes just one. We would do an exercise, then everyone would read what he or she had written and we, or I, would talk about how it could be better—only rarely did they actually rewrite.

In the third year I was there, I had the same eight students every time, a few of whom I'd had previously. Because they could get away with almost anything, my class had become somewhat of a club to them. One day we were doing an exercise I had seen about feeling like an outcast, called the Black Sheep. As I was explaining the exercise, asking if they'd ever felt that way and how you would convey such a feeling concretely, it hit me how inherently wrong this sounded. I became embarrassed. Suddenly, the kids all started talking as if I hadn't said anything, and I blushed without telling them to stop. An eighth grader who sat to my right chuckled and said, under his breath, "You mean like every day."

Still, my confidence increased exponentially. Interacting with frank critics was helping my voice as well. I found I liked being able to say I taught, even though it was voluntary and only part-time. When I came into town for it, I went to my mother's house first to drop off the dogs, and the change in atmosphere was so abrupt it felt like the two places were on different planets. I liked moving between them however.

26

I sat on top of Will in our mother's womb, causing me to be born with too much blood and him not enough. That was the first time they took blood out of one of us and put it in the other. The other time being my surgery in New Orleans. As babies, Will and I would stop crying only if our parents put us in the same crib.

Every stage of life we'd gone through not just together but as a unit, as a unity. Which makes it less surprising that after my stroke—and especially after my predicted death—things changed. Our twinship wasn't broken, but it was redefined, physically and in ways that were harder to pin down. For one thing, Will had prepared himself for me to die, and you can't completely backpedal from that once you've done it. He wouldn't say that, necessarily, but how could he not have done so? His abrupt reactions when I was in the hospital—that was part of his separating himself. His reality changed: all the outside hopes and expectations, familial and otherwise, that people had felt about us, that had been distributed equally between us, were now all on him, with the added burden that he couldn't avoid feeling responsible for me.

As I became more patient—in an effort to preserve my sanity—Will became more impatient. After he entered the workforce, he started having panic attacks. He got past them, but while they lasted, I knew they had something to do with feeling alone. He wasn't used to it.

And yet the more life told him he was now an isolated individual—Will loves to tell the story of how, after our parents discovered my enthusiasm for writing, they gave me a signed first-edition copy of Faulkner's *The Reivers* as a Christmas gift, and gave him a picture book titled *The World of Beer*—the more biology told him he wasn't. His ending up with an ex-girlfriend of mine gave him, I think, a strange sense of calm. It suggested that biological destiny might be more powerful even than something as traumatic as what had happened to my body. The accident opened him up. We got to a place, after a period of years, where we were able to discuss what had happened to me, with a candor that would have been unfamiliar to both of us before my stroke. He let go a little.

For me, although I had always loved Will as a brother (or maybe I shouldn't even say that; it would be like pointing out that I'd loved myself), I came to value him in a more conscious way, because thanks to him I had someone in my life who knew me so well, so exactly, that he could see into my interior self, regardless of what shape my body was in. Because of Will I still felt known. He could see the world through my eyes. This kept me from total despair.

I distinctly remember a period of about five seconds, when I was in a wheelchair at one of the treatment centers, thinking how much easier it would be to just become what a lot of strangers already thought I was. Overly friendly, mentally challenged. People would be nicer. I've noticed that a lot of people feel more comfortable around me the more handicapped they think I am; I suppose it's because I represent no threat. Often when I tell them something positive about myself, such as that I've had my work published or that I teach creative writing, they instantly become less friendly, as if I've forgotten my place. It would be so convenient, in a way, to go along with that attitude. But having Will there—someone who saw me as I saw myself, who knew I hadn't become someone else—gave me the strength not to take the idea too seriously, to let it pass unexplored. It can be hard to explain how frustrating it is, in my situation—someone's who's mentally there, but physically hampered, his voice changed—to have to be constantly proving yourself, insisting on what you are, and because of Will there's always one person with whom I never feel the need to do that, to waste time breaking even. Besides myself, that is. When I'm alone, I forget.

27

My sister called on a Friday in March—the twentieth, according to my journal, though when I look at the calendar, that was a Saturday. I must have been confused about either the day or the date. She said she was calling to tell me not to block the garage if I came home. But she knew I wasn't coming home that day. The real reason for her call was that she and my mother were on their way to the doctor's office, to discuss my mother's MRI results. The doctor had called and requested the meeting. Her leg had been hurting her for a while— she'd even begun using one of my father's old canes—and either we or the pain had finally convinced her to go to a doctor. They didn't know anything more, my sister said, than that he wanted to see her in his office. At first I thought, how typical of her, to get me worried over nothing. I was imagining the laugh Will and I would have over yet another example of my sister's thriving on bad news, when she called back crying. My mother had a mass on her hip, she said, and tumors up and down her spine.

I don't want to sound callous—as if the news of my mother's cancer wasn't the most jarring part of my sister's call—but I had been through so much loss in my life by then, and among my first thoughts was *I can't believe this is happening to me.* Or, worse than that, *Again?* Partly it had to do with control. Placing this new shock in the unbelievable pattern of things that had happened to me before I'd even turned thirty-seven was a way of distancing myself, making it into a story. Whatever it was, I knew that my life had just entered another new phase. I couldn't speak for a minute. I said, "I'm on my way home."

It didn't take me long to pack a few clothes and load the dogs up, but when I got to the house, her lawyer had already visited. He was just leaving. I wanted to scoff but didn't. She was simply trying to stay on top of things. I regret what I said as soon as I saw her almost as much as I do that time when I told her thanks for life and money. I think I was trying to lighten the moment. I know that I wasn't trying to be cruel. "Well," I said, "at least now you know you're not in ultimate control of your body. Are you scared?" She stared at me for a second before she started crying. "I don't want to die," she said.

My sister motioned for me to step out in the hall. She said, "Dr. Jones wants you to call him."

Dr. Jones was my doctor as well as my mother's. We were well acquainted, thanks to my many falls. He said they were going to biopsy the mass on the following Tuesday, and that we really wouldn't know anything more until then. But he also said he would be surprised if it was not malignant, quickly adding that there are many different grades of malignancy. "This could be easily treatable."

The distance that began to develop right away between my mother and reality nauseated me. She was now the patient. It put me in mind of my own days in the hospital and how much I'd hated such a designation, other people putting it on me, whereas she seemed almost to embrace it. Before she went in for the biopsy, which would require a few days' stay in the hospital, she hired a sitter and had a hospital bed installed in the front study of her house. All of it felt like a performance.

The sitter went with her to the hospital. I went back to the farm after the procedure, which they described as successful. She was recovering in the hospital. I tried rereading some of my favorite stories and essays, trying to get back into the mind-set where this wasn't the end of the world. My mother's condition was harmless. I told myself that I knew it, deep down, but I was caught up and scared. With her gift for looking the other way, you would have thought she was on vacation, having whatever she wanted brought to her and gossiping on the phone. But I knew she was scared as well.

One day the previous fall, after I'd moved from the lake to the farm, I got an e-mail message from Eleanor.

She had a different last name, but I knew right away it was her. "I bet you thought you'd never hear from me again," she wrote. She told me generally about her life over the past years. She was married to a guy she'd dated in college, who was from Chicago. She lived there with him and their two daughters. He was also a graduate of NOLS, the same program she and I met on—he'd done a semester in the Rockies in 1989. She told me she now ran marathons competitively. "Okay, now your turn," she wrote. The phrase seemed like a jolt of her former assertiveness and trust coming through. The news that she was married with children didn't bother me. I would have been surprised to learn otherwise. Mainly I was just ecstatic to hear from her.

We began trading e-mails. At first they held a sense of possibility for me, a feeling that maybe the past wasn't completely past. Not that I hoped she'd leave her husband or anything like that, but it seemed there could still be something between us. Soon, though, our back-and-forth started to feel obligatory. With the perspective of years, the fact that we'd only ever spent a little more than a month in each other's presence became apparent—especially given the consequences of the stroke. We were "different people." Neither of us seemed upset about this. It was the way things had unfolded.

But stubbornness was something she and I had in common, so we made plans to meet in Chicago, where my college roommate lived and where I would occasionally visit. We chose the dates months in advance, before I knew

anything about my mother's illness. But now she was sick,
or we feared so—she'd been released from the hospital
where they'd performed the biopsy, but we hadn't yet gone
to see the oncologist about the results. The approaching
weekend with Eleanor took on ominous overtones. I made
sure before the biopsy that my mother was still okay with
my going. She said, "Don't be silly."

When I came into town on the Thursday before I left,
I heard her hysterically laughing as soon as I walked in
the front door. It was the middle of the day and the sun
was shining. She was sitting up in the hospital bed watching the TV, and the uniformed sitter was knitting oblivi-
ously in a recliner opposite her. On the screen was one of
the first commercials for Progressive Insurance, the ads in
which the supposed customers stand on the white floor
of a mock showroom with a white background. A jaunty,
apron-wearing actress was leading the group around to
the different policies and trying to be clever. The setting
gave the whole thing an ethereal, idea-of-heaven feel, but
the humor played to the lowest common denominator—
it played on the premise that everyone was ignorant except
for you and Progressive—and wasn't even funny for that.
My mother had tears in her eyes.

"Have you seen this?" she said.

As I was leaving to go to the airport the next day, when
I went in to tell her bye, she said, "Where are you going?"
My automatic thought was to wonder if her brain had
been affected as well, then to remind myself how much
had been on her mind recently.

"Chicago," I said. "Remember? It's just for the weekend."

She looked scared. "You're not really going, are you?"

I told her it was too late to change my plans, though we both knew it wasn't. I then said that Eleanor had made dinner reservations for us, as if those, too, would be binding. Finally, I said, "Mom, please don't do this to me."

The last bit of resilience seemed to leave her. I'd beaten her, but suddenly I wasn't sure I shouldn't have let her win.

"Do you really want me to stay here?" I said.

With a crinkled nose, she just shook her head.

I knew as soon as Eleanor got to my roommate's apartment to pick me up that whatever had been between us wasn't there anymore. She knew it, too, and I could tell by the way she hurriedly began talking, asking my roommate questions without waiting for the answers, that she had expected me to look more like I'd used to (and my letters had apparently led her to believe). She was trying not to betray her disappointment. She didn't look identical to seventeen years before, either—she was skinnier (from running, she said), and more angular—but the change in my appearance was a lot more drastic. Living alone and rarely seeing people who hadn't seen me in a while, I could become unaware that I'd once looked different. I didn't feel different.

Throughout our uneventful meal and then at a local coffee shop afterward, we both seemed to be trying to make the present and the past cohere. But they were just too distinct. A few inconsequential confidences were shared, but I think we both knew that this was it. When we said goodbye, I kissed her cheek. At least I think I did. I'm sure I did. We promised to stay in touch, and kept it up for a while, but in a way you could tell was going to fade.

When I got back home that Sunday, my mother was a different person. I noticed it in how she dealt with the on-call nurse. Whereas before, when the woman had first shown up, my mother had uneasily laughed about it, saying probably she wouldn't need too much help, now the assistance was necessary. My mother was in pain.

That night, I got into a physical confrontation with my sister, who to my mind was acting like a newly appointed matriarch, addressing me as if I were her son. Having learned from my mother, she treated the whole thing like a performance, and now she had the lead. I told her that she was a terrible sister, and she slapped me in the face. The sitter called Will to come break us up. We hadn't even been to see the oncologist yet, and already the end seemed near.

Even in her condition, my mother did everything she could to change or postpone the appointment. People say that not knowing is the worst part, but for her, it was much better than knowing, since it at least allowed for hope. Everyone else wanted to get the results, so treatment could begin as soon as possible. It almost seemed that the progression of my mother's cancer accelerated after the initial diagnosis was made.

A long, silent walk, first along the corridor from the

parking deck, then across an atrium to the elevators that went up to the oncologist's office, did nothing to help the feeling that we were en route to her execution. She was sitting in a wheelchair, and her face was expressionless.

When she said she had to go to the bathroom before we went into the office, I felt that I was going to be sick as well. I was right there with her. But the oncologist happened to meet us out in the open area by the restrooms. This seemed to be a good sign—we would get the visit over with here.

He spent some time organizing the folder that had my mother's test results in it, and asked if he could feel where the hip mass had been. I saw how scared my mother was, because although she'd always been prim and proper and harped on etiquette, she stood up and dropped her pants right there. He felt around her pelvis, saying nothing.

He asked if we had any questions. Our faces must have looked confused—he hadn't told us anything yet. We'd evidently run into him before he was prepared. "I'll get together with Dr. Joncs to discuss a treatment plan," he said.

My sister asked about chemotherapy, saying she knew it had "come a long way" (Will and I glanced at each other). What could we expect there? Would she lose her hair?

He replied that, given the wide area over which the cancer had spread, they would start with the general chemotherapy that had been around since the seventies. He let that answer the second question, about the hair. After a moment, he looked at Will and me and said, "These aren't party drugs."

After the appointment I went back to the farm with the dogs, assuming the oncologist wouldn't be speaking with Dr. Jones until the next day at the soonest, so I was immediately put on alert when Will called me that afternoon. He said he'd just gotten off the phone with Dr. Jones, who himself had just spoken with the oncologist, and they had decided not even to start chemotherapy. The cancer was already so far gone, treating her would likely do more harm than good, especially with medicine that takes you to the brink of death anyway. I paused. I thought about my mother, and knew without asking that she must have felt relieved when they'd told her. The prospect of chemo was, for her, worse than anything. When I asked Will how long they thought she had, he said Dr. Jones hadn't given him a number. "He just said it should be quick."

A few days later—a week?—I went in to see her. The sitter had just stepped out of the room. I couldn't believe the decline. She was sleeping most of the time and taking an oral solution of concentrated morphine, for which I had to sign two different forms to pick up from the pharmacy. Her face was withered, and she had the same "tiny" eyes that Will gets when he's drunk. She was awake, though. This time I did somewhat better on my opening comment. Taking her hand, I said, "There's nothing to be afraid of."

She hoarsely whispered that, because of me, she wasn't. She added, "I'm gonna miss you."

To keep from crying in her face, I blurted out, "I'm not going anywhere!" . . . that, instead of all the things I might have said, that I thought of later.

Her head fell back on the pillow and she closed her eyes.

I'm not sure how much time passed between that moment and the actual end, but I can't picture her alive after that. I don't think I ever talked to her again, or at least never talked to her alone again.

One other memory of that time: there was a night when Will and my sister went into the study and my mother, waking up partway, screamed at them for keeping her alive.

Then early one morning the sitter called up the stairs, "Clay, you need to come down. Your mother has passed."

It wasn't until after I'd gone to the bathroom and begun to brush my teeth that I wondered if I should just have gone straight downstairs, if anyone was expecting me. I could hear Will climbing the stairs over the sound of the faucet. He barged into the bathroom, to see how I was taking the news. When he saw that I was fine, he almost smiled as he took in a breath, as if to say, "Well, here it is."

What he said was "What now?"

28

Nothing is left to you at this moment but to burst
out into a loud laugh. You have accomplished a
final turning and in very truth know that when a
cow in Kuai-chou grazes the herbage, a horse in
I-chou finds its stomach filled.

—YUN-AN P'U-YEN, 1156–1226

In the hospital—that is, during my own stay, after they
first said I would die, and then remain paralyzed
from my eyes down—I had this liberating flash of vision,
feeling . . . knowing. At first I didn't make much of it. This
wasn't a near-death experience; it came from out of
nowhere, when I'd slipped into thinking that none of what
was happening to me was real, and since this experience
had nothing to do with the external world, or even with
words or images, I had lumped it in with everything else,
with everything I'd imagined. But I couldn't forget it.

It happened in an instant but seemed somehow also
to occur in geological time. My first impulse is to compare
it to a glacier calving, a giant chunk of ice falling off,

something that had been building for eons and then happened. My peripheral vision jumped out to where there was no longer anything—my skin, other surfaces, the distance between them—separating me from anything else. I'd gradually stopped being aware of my unresponsive body, but now I was at the core of an infinitely expanded being. This wasn't a thought, or even a chain of thoughts. It was too seamless to allow time for thinking. But I felt it—the biggest release of my life. Release not just from the stress of being unable to move or speak, but from myself. From my self. It felt like I'd bloomed.

Unlike with morphine, this wasn't passive; nothing from outside my body was being introduced. This was active, like an orgasm, but less concentrated, and a thousand times stronger. It was as if a tinted shade I'd never known was there had been lifted. I said before that the experience wasn't composed of words or images, but there was an underlying cerebral aspect to it, an accompanying knowledge, like knowing how to breathe. It was a culmination of everything I'd learned in my life before then and a simultaneous disregarding of it. My dramatic idea of myself still existed, and had the same setup as always: me writing a script, acting it out, and watching from the audience at the same time. But the walls that had separated them were gone. I fully became each and all of them, as well as everything else—good and bad. I had the vivid sense, too, that this had always been the case. It had never been me against anything. It dawned on me not that everything was *going to be* okay, but that everything *was* okay.

The clarity I felt was like becoming decongested. It was that close to my normal perception.

From later reading, I learned that people of all backgrounds, cultures, and religions, throughout history, have had versions, in varying degrees, of the same experience, of what I'd taken to calling my "willing elimination of options." In his essay "This Is It" the philosopher Alan Watts says, "the experience has a tendency to arise in situations of total extremity or despair, when the individual finds himself without any alternative but to surrender himself entirely." I smiled when I read that. This *was* it. I knew I wasn't crazy.

I had already surrendered my body soon after I got to the hospital, but only by letting go of my desire to live or to die—to control my existence—could I surrender entirely. Doing so was not conscious. The experience felt both like I'd willed it and like it had come out of nowhere. I became my will—there was nothing holding me back anymore—but *my will* was more than me. As an identical twin, I'd always thought along these lines, but now it was made certain. It didn't seem strange how refreshed and unafraid I felt, just inevitable.

29

I t took longer than Dewin thought it would before I could actually sing a song—and certainly my voice has a ways to go—but over the years of weekly lessons, it has noticeably improved. The first song we attempted was "Happy Birthday," which was challenging enough at first. It felt different than just doing the exercises. The song imparted rhythm, and that was useful—people talk in rhythm.

A few months ago, we started going through the aria "Ah! Tu Non Sai" from Handel's *Ottone*. Just writing the title makes the whole thing sound suspect. Who was I kidding? But as opera songs go, it's fairly straightforward. It follows a pattern, and it flows.

The song is in Italian, too, which Dewin had mentioned is more conducive to singing than English. Not as many rough transitions. Dewin let me see an English translation of the words. A woman, Matilda, is pleading with the emperor to release her lover from prison.

> Ah! you know not how my heart is rent,
> Nor the pity I feel, nor the pain.
> After all the sorrowful hours we've spent
> I would still see him free again!

In 1723 Handel wrote Matilda's aria specially for the English contralto Anastasia Robinson, who hadn't liked the role when first presented with it. She asked for something more subdued, more suited to her gifts. Handel agreed, a sign of the esteem in which he held her voice, and wrote "Ah! Tu Non Sai" for her. A curious thing about Anastasia Robinson is that she started her career as an alto, but contracted smallpox, evidently around 1719. The disease damaged her voice in a way that limited its range, and when she reemerged, it was different, lower. Handel wrote "Ah! Tu Non Sai" for her second, damaged voice. I don't know if Dewin knew this when he decided to have me sing it.

A benefit born of necessity, in working with Dewin, is that I've picked up a rudimentary knowledge of reading music. Still, I have trouble with the actual singing, particularly when there's an abrupt shift in registers. But now there are moments when I find myself experiencing the song as an organic unit, one composed of separate parts, and not as a series of parts lined up in a row. That subtle shift in feeling has marked a huge step for me. There's a letter John Irving sent to Kurt Vonnegut in 1982. "Your books always create the perfect illusion," Irving wrote, "that you know exactly all those parts of the story as you are telling us just one of the parts, and that simply makes everything sound true. You have to be a writer to feel that." I think the same is true of singing.

At first, when I couldn't get all the way through a certain section, when I didn't think I had the breath, Dewin would play a kind of trick on me: he would have me silently mouth the words, proceeding note by note, "just to get the coordination down." It was clever, on his part—by forcing me to keep moving my mouth, beyond what I'd assumed was the limit of my breath, he showed me that in fact I had more air than I knew.

"Notice how many times we come back to E," Dewin said, when we got to the song's middle section. "Let that be your base."

Something was wrong. I was reaching the notes in time, but the sound wasn't right. I would open my mouth, and the notes . . . it wasn't that they would get cut off, so much as that they would never start, while the background music kept running.

"What am I doing?" I asked in frustration.

"Your voice is wanting to shut down when you close around the consonants," Dewin answered. "It's saying, 'That's it, we're done.' But you've got to keep the sound open, to keep the flow going."

We tried just those words a few more times.

"It's still not sounding right," I told him. "When I try to imitate you, it doesn't even sound like the same song."

Dewin smiled. "You're not being vulnerable," he said. "This person's heart is broken . . . You've heard your dogs whine? That 'mmh, mmh, mmh.' That's . . ."

"Yeah, like when they dream?"

"Yeah, that's sincere vulnerability. That's how you sing. If you sing properly, the acoustics . . . it's so natural you're only involved in letting it take your body. People associate the emotional impact of singing because they hear that connectivity."

A few years earlier, I might have pointed out to him that this was an example of faith, but not of the sort we usually mean by that word. It was the kind of faith that is so basic, life isn't possible without it. I almost said that. But it's like the Zen master Chokei once told a monk, outside their temple. The monk had said, "Right here is the peak of the mystic mountain. Is not this Reality?"

"So it is," Chokei replied, "but what a pity to say so."

I knew afterward, driving home, that this had been one of my better lessons. My voice felt strong and full of potential—I was learning to count on it when I opened my mouth, and no longer had to use all my strength just to make it heard. I felt a pleasant surprise when speaking to a cashier, in feeling the words come out with effort to spare, even if I was winded.

When I got home, the phone was ringing. I had to walk all the way across the "barn" room to get it. It was my sister, and I could tell by the way she said "Hey!"—vaguely caught off guard but not enough to pursue the matter—that she'd assumed, from how I'd answered, that I was Will. She started talking about Betsy and the girls, saying something about their school, which her daughter also attended at the time. She asked a few simple questions that didn't require more than a yes or a no, or if one did, I would carefully say, "I don't know," and she would go on. I was only half-listening at that point. I wondered how long it would be before she figured out who I really was.

Acknowledgments

I'd like to thank my agent and fellow Sewanee alum, Amy Hughes, for taking this on, and Emily Bell at FSG for the same, as well as everyone else I've worked with at FSG, specifically Donna Cheng for the cover design. Blanche Fields, Nancy Allen, Trae and Colton Hawkins, Dewin Tibbs, Betsy Byars, Frank and Laurie Jones, Charles Clayton, Katherine Berdy, Brother Phillips, Jay Dismukes, Parker Evans, James Hollingsworth, Grey Ingram, Charles Crommelin, Stephen Walker, Jay Spencer, David Bowman, Brys and Zoë Stephens, Serena Vann, Barbara Major, Stephen Jackson, Mimi Bittick, Emily Chenoweth, Chip and Elizabeth Brantley, Milo Ryan, John Boyd, Jack Strifling, Winslow Hastie, Hampton Logan, B. T. Thomas, Edward Carlos, George Stevenson, Andrew McCalla, Jim Johnston,

Tommy Kendrick, Caroline Reynolds, Jane Cooper, Amy Dillard, Priscilla Stokes, Michael Seale, Stutts and Jill Everette, Tracy Thomas, Casey Whiting, and Jennifer Desiderio have also all been instrumental in one way or another, as has David Kline. Special thanks to Lathrop Smith and family, Sarah Brolyes, Will Minton, Brett Connor, Michael Croft, Michael Terrell, Matt Murphree, Michael O'Rorke, and to everyone at the Sewanee School of Letters, especially John Grammer, Meg Binnicker, April Alvarez, Ellen Slezak, Elizabeth Skomp, Andrew Hudgins, Chris Bachelder, and Holly Goddard Jones, as well as to my doctors and therapists at Spain and Lakeshore rehabs. Special thanks also to Robert Pearigen and Paul Engsberg. Finally, I am eternally grateful for my work and friendship with Wyatt Prunty, Tom Jenks, and John Jeremiah Sullivan, without whom this book wouldn't exist. Special thanks to Joel Finsel and John's family as well.